SwingOut

Great Negro Dance Bands

by Gene Fernett

PENDELL
PUBLISHING
COMPANY

Library of Congress Catalog Card Number: 78-98066

Table of Contents

INTRODUCTION

PROLOGUE

1. THE NEGRO BRINGS JAZZ TO THE BIG BAND AGE 11
2. FATE MARABLE 17
3. JIM EUROPE AND THE HELLFIGHTERS 19
4. FLETCHER HENDERSON 21
5. CHARLIE COOK 25
6. DUKE ELLINGTON 29
7. MC KINNEY'S COTTON PICKERS 37
8. ALPHONSO TRENT 41
9. NOBLE SISSLE 45
10. COUNT BASIE 49
11. SPEED WEBB AND HIS HOLLYWOOD BLUE DEVILS 57
12. LOUIS ARMSTRONG AND THE BIG BANDS 61
13. CHICK WEBB AND HIS CHICKS 65
14. ELLA FITZGERALD AND HER ORCHESTRA 69
15. FATS WALLER 73
16. ANDY KIRK AND HIS CLOUDS OF JOY 77
17. ERSKINE HAWKINS 83
18. DON REDMAN 93
19. THE JETER-PILLARS BAND 97
20. LIONEL HAMPTON 101
21. CAB CALLOWAY 103
22. CLAUDE HOPKINS 109
23. JIMMIE LUNCEFORD 111
24. HARLAN LEONARD AND HIS ROCKETS 115
25. EARL "FATHA" HINES 119
26. DIZZY GILLESPIE 123
27. AND OTHER VOICES* 125
28. CAN THE BIG BANDS RETURN? 169

INDEX

*See following page for complete listing of the "other voices".

AND ALL THE "OTHER VOICES" (HERE LISTED IN ALPHABETICAL ORDER):

- LEON ABBEY
- SHUFFLE ABERNATHY
- JASPER "JAP" ALLEN
- WALTER BARNES AND HIS ROYAL CREOLIANS
- EUBIE BLAKE AND HIS "SHUFFLE ALONG" ORCHESTRA
- TINY BRADSHAW
- WILLIE BRYANT
- BILLY BUTLER (THE SAVOY BEARCATS)
- ELMER CALLOWAY
- BENNY CARTER
- CHIC CARTER
- CHRIS COLUMBUS' MAD MEN
- CHARLIE CREATH
- BILLY ECKSTINE
- ROY ELDRIDGE
- CHARLIE ELGAR'S DREAMLAND AND MUNICIPAL PIER ORCHESTRA
- MERCER ELLINGTON
- JOE GARLAND
- W.C. HANDY
- MARION HARDY'S ALABAMIANS
- COLEMAN HAWKINS
- TEDDY HILL
- LES HITE
- DOC HYDER
- ALEX JACKSON
- DEWEY JACKSON
- BUDDY JOHNSON
- LOUIS JORDAN
- MILTON LARKINS
- GEORGE E. LEE AND HIS NOVELTY SINGING ORCHESTRA
- JAY MC SHANN
- LUCKY MILLINDER
- MILLS BLUE RHYTHM
- GEORGE MORRISON
- BENNIE MOTEN'S KANSAS CITY ORCHESTRA
- JOE "KING" OLIVER'S DIXIE SYNCOPATORS
- RENAISSANCE BALLROOM ORCHESTRA
- ELI RICE
- LUCKEY ROBERTS
- ALLIE ROSS
- LUIS RUSSELL'S SARATOGA CLUB ORCHESTRA
- WILBUR SWEATMAN
- THE SWEETHEARTS OF RHYTHM
- ERSKINE TATE'S VENDOME THEATRE ORCHESTRA
- J. FRANK TERRY'S CHICAGO NIGHTINGALES
- FESS WHATLEY
- ZACK WHYTE AND HIS CHOCOLATE BEAU BRUMMELS
- COOTIE WILLIAMS
- FESS WILLIAMS AND HIS ROYAL FLUSH ORCHESTRA
- TEDDY WILSON
- SAM WOODING

Dedication

To Andy Kirk, without whose help the book A THOUSAND GOLDEN HORNS would have been difficult to produce, and this volume virtually impossible.

Gene Fernett

Acknowledgements

Collecting the photographs and stories for this volume was a major task which, happily for the author, was made pleasant through the kind help of a good many wonderful persons in and out of the music field.

As with the author's first volume, A THOUSAND GOLDEN HORNS, it is impossible to thank all those who aided in preparing this book. Here, however, are some who deserve special thanks:

• *Mrs. Essie Mae Trent*, for photos of, and information about, her late husband Alphonso Trent and his orchestra;

• *Mr. J. L. McDaniel*, the remarkably skilled photographer at Tiffany Studios, Cocoa, Florida, who re-copied many of the rare and priceless photos used herein;

• *Mr. S. Lawrence "Speed" Webb*, who supplied many valuable photos and most of the information on his fine orchestra;

• *Mr. T. D. Kemp, Jr.*, for the excellent photos of young Louis Armstrong;

• *Mr. Harry Dial* who, as one of the last living members of the early Fate Marable riverboat orchestras, opened both his pleasant memories and his photo collection to the author;

• *Mr. Billy Butler*, for the valuable material on Charles Cook, the Cook's Dreamland Orchestra, *et al*;

• *Mr. Andy Kirk*, for the Marion Hardy pictures, and all the photos of the Andy Kirk Clouds of Joy;

• *Erskine Hawkins*, for much information on his orchestra;

• *Mr. Harold Blanchard*, for help in preparing the section on Teddy Hill;

• *Mr. Francis Williams*, for much information on, and several photos of, Duke Ellington, Ella Fitzgerald and the Frank Terry band;

• *Mr. Taft Jordan*, who gave the author invaluable information on the Chick Webb and Doc Hyder bands;

• *Mr. Harlan Leonard*, for a large portion of the material on his orchestra, the Rockets;

• *Roseland Dance City*, for photos of the original Roseland Ballroom;

• *Mr. Jerry Miller*, of RCA Victor, for letting the author conduct a little supervised "raid" on the photo file;

• *Mr. Julian Dash*, for the photo of the entire Erskine Hawkins band;

• *Mr. Haywood Henry*, for more fine photos in the book than can be readily counted;

• *Mrs. Don Redman*, for photos and information concerning her late husband and his orchestra;

• *Mr. Cyril Little*, and *Hershey Park* (Pa.) for several of the Basie, Hampton and Ellington photos;

• *Mr. George Hamid* and the *Steel Pier* (N.J.) for still further Basie and Ellington pictures;

• *St. Louis Globe-Democrat*, and its Associate Managing Editor, Mr. Martin L. Duggan, for the splendid photos of the riverboats;

• *Mr. Noble Sissle*, for rare old photographs of his orchestra, and for much of the material utilized in the chapter on his musical career;

• *Mr. Julian Hensley*, for countless photos of such bands as Tiny Bradshaw, Buddy Johnson and others;

• *International Musician*, for the views of Lionel Hampton's big band, and several other photos;

• *Mr. Ray Copeland*, for pictures of the Chris Columbus and the Mercer Ellington aggregations;

• *Mr. Leon Abbey*, for photos and factual data on his orchestra;

• *Mr. James Jeter*, who patiently helped the author assemble the story of the Jeter-Pillars band;

• *Mr. George Morrison*, who provided the background material on his band;

• *Mr. Demas Dean*, who proffered a wealth of information on, and supplied two rare pictures of the Savoy Bearcats;

• *Mr. Langston W. Curl*, who added much data to our chapter on McKinney's Cotton Pickers;

• *Mr. Duncan Schiedt*, who once again came up with a number of photographic gems from his seemingly bottomless treasure chest of such material;

• *Mr. Sam Wooding*, for the picture and the material on his band;

• *Mr. Eubie Blake*, that charming pioneer of Tin Pan Alley and the American musical theatre, for the wonderful Jim Europe picture, and other photos;

- *Mr. Edgar Sampson*, for the very excellent Chick Webb photo and the personnel identification of the band;

- *Mr. Moses Allen*, the talented bass player, and one of the original members of the Jimmie Lunceford band, for checking the Lunceford chapter for accuracy;

- *Mr. John T. Whatley*, for photos of his orchestras;

- *Mr. Ed Burke*, for information regarding the Walter Barnes band;

- *Mr. Joe Mason*, of WGY, Schenectady, for the excellent photo of Walter Barnes and his Royal Creolians;

- *Mr. Bertrand Demeusy*, the distinguished French jazz writer and collector, for several photos included herein;

- *Mr. Fred Norman*, for the Elmer Calloway and Claude Hopkins photos.

. . . and the many other music enthusiasts who took the time to aid the author in his research, preparation, and editing of the material in this volume.

Gratefully,

Gene Fernett

Cocoa, Florida
1967

INTRODUCTION
Just How Great Is Great

The very title of this book may appear to be a misnomer to many who stop to study it. What, exactly, is meant by the word "great" in the title, they may wonder. What criteria were used in selecting the orchestras included in this volume?

Just as the search for a universal definition of the word "jazz" will set semanticists, musicologists, and jazz musicians to arguing, so too will the author's use of the adjective "great" as a part of the title of this work.

To find inclusion in this volume a bandleader and his musical group had to meet one or more of the following criteria:

- To have achieved a measure of fame which endured for some time;
- To have included personnel and musical arrangements, or to have made musical contributions to American dance music (or to jazz per se) which place the band in a league with the most important orchestras of the period in which the subject was prominent;
- To have comprised regular, travelling personnel numbering 10 persons or upward;
- To have recorded several phonograph records which might thus imply, at least, a wide acceptance of the group, musically.

As with the author's first book, A THOUSAND GOLDEN HORNS, this work makes no attempt to differentiate between jazz bands and the so-called "commercial" groups. Jazz in its heyday was, for the most part, dance music. If we accept this fact,

then the difference between a "jazz" band and a "commercial" one becomes of minimal importance, at least so far as this book is concerned. GREAT NEGRO DANCE BANDS is an attempt to chronicle an era of American musical history with a degree of accuracy difficult to achieve. There are, after all, few written historical data relating to Negro dance bands of our nation. Moreover, the bandleaders of such groups, travelling the country as they did, dealing with thousands of problems inherent in operating their organizations, seldom had time to write down detailed records. As a result, the writer who chooses such a task as the one represented herein must painstakingly seek out the sidemen who worked in those bands. He must make detailed studies of discographies, obituaries, scanty and "slanted" record album "notes" and similar written material. More importantly, he must visit band bookers, musical arrangers, even the relatives of the musicians, checking and re-checking details. Sometimes, heaven forbid!, he must even rely upon the most undependable source of all—pure hearsay, if such a thing is ever "pure".

One final word: This book is by no means an attempt to catalog all the many Negro bands of past and present. It is not even an effort to bring together only the big bands in which talented Negroes have served. It is, instead, one man's very eclectic volume about an adventuresome era of American dance music.

Prologue

Over the span of roughly half a century which has passed since World War I, countless dance orchestras have blazed across the skies of musical America. Some have been mere meteorites, flaming brightly even as they fell toward sudden ends. Others have been brilliant, steady stars, fixed in the heavens and seemingly timeless.

Among those musical galaxies were innumerable Negro bands, those spirited and fiercely proud clans who defied the apathy of audiences too long inured to hotel bands with muffled brass and muddy beat.

There is an inexplicable magic about the Negro bands. Although some of them suffered from faulty intonation and a raggedness of phrasing which approached the first throes of pure anarchy, many others were far superior to the white bands with which they competed.

And what those bands may have lacked in precision, they more than made up for in enthusiasm! There was a drive, a spirit to a Negro orchestra which pitifully few white bands ever achieved, an indefinable rapport that gave even the casual listener the impression that playing in one of these groups must have been sheer adventure—which frequently it was!

And while those Negro bands were making themselves heard, they taught their white contemporaries much which eventually improved all dance music: Jo Jones showed every big band drummer how much better was the beat when kicked along on the high hat instead of the foot pedal of the bass drum; Jimmie Lunceford demonstrated how much a big band could be improved with slick, precision use of flashing mutes. And Sy Oliver, Lunceford's star arranger, showed everyone, white and colored, how beefy, strutting arrangements, coupled with a powerhouse brass section, could generate a million volts of excitement—a couple facts which men such as Tommy Dorsey carried straight down to the savings bank!

Delightful showmen and skilled performers who played with "soul," the Negro bands (whether they knew it or not at the time) were also a force in breaking down racial barriers. For to many a white American of twenty, thirty, or forty years ago, his first knowledge of the Negro's immense talents and considerable abilities came from seeing and hearing the Negro big bands.

When all these facts are considered, this book becomes something more than a collection of photographs and stories; it is a record of progress and achievement against odds almost unbelievable today.

It is a record to which the men of those orchestras may rightfully point with immense and honest pride.

New York's old Roseland Ballroom, spacious, yet only about half the size of the present-day Roseland Dance City on 52nd Street. These photos, taken some time between 1920 and 1930, reveal a decor of ruffled silk and heavy ornateness quite typical of the period. In this setting, the original Fletcher Henderson band and numerous other Negro orchestras set thousands of dancing feet into action. The signs above the double bandstand reveal that, on the day this photo was taken, the white band being featured was that of Harvey Marburger. The colored band, on the same program, was that of Fletcher Henderson!

Completely redecorated in 1930, Roseland (then situated at the northeast corner of Broadway and 51st Street) still retained the hand-decorated silk ceiling patterns which had similarly adorned the place as part of the original decor. When Fletcher Henderson reorganized his band in 1935, this is one of the first ballrooms in which he played. *(Photos courtesy of Roseland Dance City)*

CHAPTER I

The Negro Brings Jazz
To The Big Band Age

The big band days were really something—but they probably wouldn't have been if jazz hadn't come on the scene.

There were great ballrooms before the 1930s, but it is doubtful that there would ever have been so many of them if it hadn't been for the Negro bands who breathed life into dance music; for exciting music, played by gifted artists, draws crowds who spend money and, in turn, induce investors to build more ballrooms.

And wherever any new ballroom was located, it was sure to possess one quality: bigness. It was a time when bigness was, in fact, almost a fetish with Americans.

It's true that we may have been driving seven or eight year-old Model A Fords then, but that was only because something called "The Great Depression" made it necessary that we do so.

It was bigness that we admired. The Empire State Building. A thousand feet into the air, with a mooring mast on top, so huge silver dirigibles could be moored at its tip.

Massive, thundering old Lincoln limousines. Twelve cylinder Packards.

Long, low 1937 Cord cars. Front wheel drive, with massive V8 Lycoming engines, and dashboards filled with gleaming dials—big ones.

The kidnap of a big air hero's baby, with a spectacular Charles Lindbergh leading a clumsy chase for the kidnapper, as big headlines told of it.

The towering figure of the unbeatable "Brown Bomber" from Detroit, champion Joe Louis.

Why this penchant for impressive size?

For one thing, it helped us forget for a moment, the awesome beginnings of the German Third Reich.

Bigness to overcome our self-pity for our sorry economic condition, for race prejudice.

Big ballrooms. Big bands. Big romances.

These were at once our opiate and, at the same time, the stuff of which our hopeful dreams were woven.

This preoccupation with bigness began to assert itself in larger dance bands at about the close of World War I. By the mid-1920s, the hotel or ballroom with only a small bandstand was finding it necessary to call in carpenters to add several feet to the platform in order to accommodate the larger aggregations of musicians which were fast coming into vogue.

Some early pioneers of the big band movement were white bands such as those of Art Hickman, Walter Wolfe Kahn, Ted Fio Rito and the like. These bands had laid the groundwork by the early 1920s.

Paul Whiteman and his talented contemporary Fletcher Henderson had by then shown how written arrangements could be applied to big bands—Whiteman through pseudo-symphonic stylings, Henderson through charts which were heavily infused with real jazz.

But from the close of World War I until the 1930s, the big band scene was dominated by several generations of all-white orchestras of the "sweet band" variety. Violins were in evidence almost everywhere. Vincent Lopez, Isham Jones and a score of others were dominant names during this sterile period of popular music.

The music had a horrible sameness about it, even though here and there a band did sometimes manage to rise above its contemporaries with a welcome bit of originality.

But generally speaking, prior to 1934, if there were any hope at all for better things in American dance music, it was held by the Negro bands of the time, principally those of Duke Ellington, Fletcher Henderson, Jimmie Lunceford and a handful of others.

Whether the band was spawned in Washington, D.C., as was Ellington's; New York, as were

Henderson's and Webb's; or came roaring in from the Midwest, as did Basie, Kirk and McKinney's Cotton Pickers, the band had two things in common with the others of its ilk: It was a Negro outfit, and it was a magnificent orchestra.

Such bands were considerably fewer in number than were the white orchestras of the time, and besides, the odds against them were multiplied by the race prejudice which was so strong that it prevented their playing in many of the really choice dance locations.

It was not always simple, either, for the Negro musician to travel to his jobs with any certainty that he would be accorded any but the very poorest of accommodations. This was as true of the North as of the South, for Northern "liberality" was so slightly greater than the Southern variety as to make the difference almost unmeasurable!

Billy Butler, that affable and light-skinned Negro, not long ago, gave a delightful account of the problems of travel incurred by his race in the 1920s.

"I was travelling with a wonderful little vaudeville troupe called 'the Shieks of Araby,' five of us, playing the big Pantages circuit," Billy begins.

"In those days, the good hotels and the high class restaurants were closed to Negroes, so we often were forced to stop overnight at rooming houses which were literally crawling with vermin. In fact, we often sought out the local house of prostitution, because it was cleaner than the other places which were open to us then."

Without a trace of bitterness, with an impish twinkle in his eye, Butler continues, "Once, up in Ohio, after a week of terrible food and worse rooms, I looked at all the 'Shieks of Araby' at the end of our performance one day and said, 'How'd you like to eat tonight in the best restaurant in town?' Of course everyone laughed at that.

"'No, I mean it,' I said. When they looked surprised, I said, 'Keep those Arab outfits on and follow me!' "

Butler walked his incredulous band of followers to the finest cafe he could find. They paused only a moment before a hugh window, beyond which stood an empty table, and above that a lovely cut-glass chandelier, adding a touch of elegance to the setting. "In here," Butler said, waving his skieks through the door, "and act like you don't speak English," he warned.

There was a hushed, reverential silence in the restaurant as the dark-skinned guests seated themselves. Had they been dressed as mere American Negroes, they would have been ejected. But now they were exotic; they were Far Easterners, and very, acceptable to the management.

"Them no speak English," Butler quickly advised the waiter, waving a sympathetic arm at his friends. The waiter nodded, handing Butler a menu as he did so.

"Me order for all," Butler reassured the bowing waiter. Then, in "stage talk" (a kind of pig Latin, but more confusing to the ear of the uninitiated) Billy asked each of the shieks, in turn, what he wanted to order. One by one, in broken English, Butler transmitted the orders. With complete alacrity, the waiter complied, and Butler was heard to breathe audibly beneath his flowing robe.

The check paid, their hungers appeased, the strange quintet next strode into the lobby of a hotel they had eyed enviously on the morning of their arrival. There, the group scored its second successful ruse of the day, and with that moment a delightful pattern was established.

"We kept those outfits well laundered from then on," says Butler, "and had plenty of changes of garb, because those things were doing double duty: On the stage for two-a-day vaudeville; as our tickets to hotels and restaurants after the shows."

Colored musicians still laugh at Billy's ingenuity, and speak gratefully of the changes in our society which gradually are making such deception largely unnecessary now. Ever so slowly, down through the years, the Negro and his music have pushed aside the boundaries of racial intolerance, and found acceptance. And in doing so, the colored musician brought his people and his kind of jazz to the world at large.

The lounge area at the first *Roseland Ballroom,* some time after the complete renovation of the famous dance center, in 1930.

A full shot of the dance floor of the old Roseland Ballroom, as it appeared between 1930 and 1956. During the latter year, the old Roseland was torn down, and replaced with a newer, larger ballroom, just two blocks away.

A sight to evoke many memories for any musician who ever was "on the road": The band bus. Besides serving as transportation for orchestras, such vehicles provided places to sleep whenever the schedule prohibited overnight stops. *(Photo by courtesy of Andy Kirk)*

Nothing, however apt, can describe the wild, wonderful antics of the jitterbugs of the 1940s. Never before and never since has dancing been half so frenzied, half so free of form — or a tenth as much fun to see or to try! (Photo courtesy N. Y. Public Library)

"Jeeterbogs are ze bonk," said the French author of the book LE JAZZ HOT, but the dancers didn't even pause when critics scoffed. The music was too hot, too exciting and, besides, who could hear the critics when five brass, four reeds and four rhythm were rocking the room?

15

A view across the spacious lower lobby of the original *Roseland Ballroom,* as it appeared during the period 1920-30. Note the "mission bells" over the staircase! (Photo by courtesy of Roseland Ballroom)

Like a giant magnet, New York City—principally the island of Manhattan—has drawn musicians who come here seeking their fortunes amid the concrete chasms. Once here, Negro artists often worked largely within the Harlem-area clubs and ballrooms which possessed such magic names as The Golden Gate, The Cotton Club, The Savoy, The Uproar House, and the Apollo Theatre. Young Chick Webb looked wonderingly at these lights when he first came from Baltimore to "The Big Apple," as New York was then known by musicians. So, too, did Andy Kirk, Count Basie, and scores of others, for success in New York often means success across the nation! (Photo courtesy RCA Victor)

CHAPTER II
Fate Marable

In the early days of jazz, the riverboats which plied the Mississippi were important sources of income for musicians, particularly those who travelled aboard the steamers out of New Orleans and St. Louis. Charlie Creath and Dewey Jackson played on those boats. So did Alphonso Trent, Louis Armstrong, and countless others. But the bandleader who had the longest association with the riverboat dance crowds undoubtedly was Fate Marable (1890 to 1947).

Marable's story was beautifully related, not long ago, by drummer Harry Dial who, by all rights, is probably one of the best authorities on Fate and his men—and on those riverboats, too.

Smiling as if recalling a sweet dream, Dial sat in his comfortable apartment high atop a favored spot on Sugar Hill in Harlem, where he has lived for close to thirty years now, and talked of Marable and the boats.

"I went to work on the boats in 1923," Dial began. "Fate had come to St. Louis with a good-sized band in 1919—10 or 11 pieces—one called 'The Metropolitan Jazz Band,' which comprised Louis Armstrong, Norman Mason, Louis Brashear, George "Pops" Foster, Johnny St. Cyr, Fate himself on piano, and Baby Dodds on drums. There was also a violinist, Boyd Atkins, and two clarinetists, Jerome Pasquale and Johnny Dodds. Norman Mason, who later switched to saxophone, was a trumpeter in that band. David Jones, at this time, played nothing but mellophone; he switched to sax later, too.

"They didn't have any special arrangements," Dial said. "They used stock music, and Fate used to cut them up and teach the guys instructions and things that he wanted. Those stocks had no banjo parts, though; those came later."

Dial also recalled how Marable used to play a steam calliope as a daily feature aboard one of the New Orleans boats—about 15 minutes or half an hour of such music—because it drew a crowd. It also drew attention to the boat itself which, as Dial described it, " . . . could be seen clear up Canal Street, all lighted up just like an apartment building, or something."

Aboard the old Streckfus steamer "J.S.," Harry Dial began touring with Fate Marable in about 1923, making "day trips"—excursions daily, upriver from St. Louis to around Alton, Illinois, and back.

"They had a beautiful dance floor aboard," Dial continued. "And those boats were kept immaculate. Streckfus steamship lines was a very progressive company."

In telling the story of his association with Marable, Dial was careful to point out that, contrary to a statement widely accepted, Fate Marable DID cut a few phonograph records for OKeh Records, in New Orleans, in 1924, among them "Frankie and Johnny," although it was Zutty Singleton, not Dial, who was the drummer on those discs, Harry Dial himself disclosed.

"Fate was one fine musician," Dial says, "who received his musical education at Straights College, in New Orleans; the Streckfus people sent him there. And he was such a good musician that long BEFORE he had his first Negro band on the boats, he was leading a 10-piece white band, whose leader had died. Those men were so fond of Fate's ability that they asked him to take over the band. He had a white band for about seven years BEFORE he had his first colored band—from maybe 1912 to 1919."

Marable's popularity with musicians and public extended, as well, to the men who owned and operated the Streckfus lines.

"Whenever Fate wanted to work, he worked. If he didn't want to go, in later years, Streckfus got another leader," Dial continued. "Most of the time, he wanted to work. But anyway, he had a standing engagement with Streckfus; he was THAT good."

In an age when the colored musician found only limited outlets for his ability, men such as Fate Marable began to tear down the stubborn wall of resistance which separated two worlds, and in so-doing, helped a bit to end long centuries of racial intolerance, by means of his talent and his music.

Mississippi steamers such as the Streckfus liner J.S. — somewhat anachronistic even by the 1920s — gave employment to many orchestras, among them Fate Marable's and Charlie Creath's bands. (Photo by courtesy of *St. Louis Globe-Democrat*)

The Fate Marable Orchestra, shown aboard the *S.S. Capitol.* Marable was one of the great riverboat bandleaders and, like his contemporary Charlie Creath, he led some outstanding bands. Marable started his career before World War I, and was still active well into the 1940s. *(Photo courtesy of Harry Dial)* PERSONNEL: Zutty Singleton, drummer, (Standing): Norman Mason, Bert Bailey, Walter Thomas, saxes; Barnett Bradley, violin; Harvey Langford, trombone; Sydney Desvignes, trumpet; Henry Kimball, tuba; Fate Marable, Piano. The banjo player is Willie Foster, the brother of "Pops" Foster.

CHAPTER III
Jim Europe And The Hellfighters

James Reese Europe was born in Mobile, Alabama, February 22, 1881, but when he was not quite ten, his family moved to Washington, D.C., where he took violin lessons. In 1904, he migrated to New York, drawn there by word of the success of the touring Negro musical companies.

Soon after his arrival, Europe found work as the director of the orchestra which accompanied a show called SHOO FLY REGIMENT, with which troupe he travelled for some three years. In 1909, however, he returned to New York, where he gave piano lessons and ultimately set about helping to organize the Clef Club, a Negro musicians' employment hall. At about the same time, he organized a large "stage band" which appeared for several years at an annual "Clef Club Concert," the first one of which was presented in 1910. A strange grouping of instruments, Europe's gigantic stage band included, at one concert, 47 mandolins, 27 harp-guitars (a guitar with seven added bass strings) 11 banjos, 8 violins, 10 pianos—and one saxophone!

When, in 1912, the 11-piece society orchestra of Jim Europe became associated with the white dance team of Vernon and Irene Castle (two former stage stars who turned dancers)* a good many Clef Club members became envious of Europe's success—some of them so much so that they more than hinted that he was using the Clef Club telephone as a booking office exclusively for Jim Europe—not for colored musicians in general. At that point, Europe walked out of the Clef Club for good, and founded a new organization of a similar nature, calling it the Tempo Club, and naming himself as its president.

Europe's society band, with its immense

*As early as 1912 James Reese Europe accompanied the Castle musical WATCH YOUR STEP, an Irving Berlin show.

publicity deriving from its association with the Castle dance team, and with its successful Victor phonograph record sales, was a tremendously profitable orchestra. In 1915 alone, Europe's booking office processed nearly a hundred thousand dollars' worth of contracts, as the Tempo Club grew to more than 200 members.

Early in 1917, James Europe enlisted in New York's Negro regiment, the Fifteenth Infantry, with a commission of lieutenant. Colonel William Haywood, commander of the regiment, asked Europe to organize a large regimental band. The resulting group, known in France as "The Hellfighters," turned out to be the best known, and the best, of the World War I military groups. A first-class marching band, the organization could be broken down into dance orchestras, as well, which it frequently was. As a military parade outfit, it was led by drum major Bill "Bojangles" Robinson, later to become famous as a tap dancer and a movie star in his own right.

When World War I ended, Europe and his band returned to New York, their triumphal parade down Fifth Avenue, February 17, 1919, drawing a million New Yorkers to watch and listen.

On May 9 of that same year, while Europe and his band were appearing at Mechanics' Hall, Boston, he was fatally stabbed by one of his own men, Private Herbert Wright, while Europe was chastising Wright for walking rudely across the stage against Europe's orders.

Jim Europe made great contributions to the betterment of the Negro musicians and to the firm establishment of the colored orchestra, both for Negro and white musical functions.

Buried with full military honors, May 14, 1919, he was only 40 years old at the time of his unfortunate passing.

An early photo of one of the "Clef Club" orchestras of James Reese Europe — in this case the 1914 version of the band. Because of Europe's early passing, relatively few pictures of him have survived. This one certainly is one of the best. (Photo by courtesy of Eubie Blake)

CHAPTER IV
Fletcher Henderson

"Every time I play a 'battle of the bands,'" Fletcher Henderson told a close friend in 1931, "I hear my arrangements coming back at me from another orchestra—arrangements I bought and paid for. But from now on," he continued, "they're not going to do it, because I'm going to do my own arranging."

And with that moment, the mild-mannered Henderson added the chores of arranging to his already-considerable duties as pianist for, and leader of, one of the most delightful and irresponsible orchestras ever assembled.

A Southerner by birth, James Fletcher Henderson retained to his death many of the slow, imperturbable traits which Cuthbert, Georgia, engendered in most of its native sons—particularly those born there in the sleepy period just before the turn of this century.

Fletcher, born December 18, 1898, was six years old when his brother Horace was born, and was already taking piano lessons from his mother—who taught music while her husband, Fletcher, Senior, worked as principal of a local high school. So, while music was an integral, continuing part of the Hendersons' home life, it was never a profession to which the parents really wanted either of their children to aspire.

So in the era of World War I, when young Fletcher went to Atlanta University to study chemistry, both parents happily predicted a bright future for their eldest son, who strengthened their faith by moving to New York City in 1920 for still further studies in the science.

Not long after he arrived in New York, Henderson took a part-time position as a piano playing "song plugger" at the W.C. Handy Music Company and in 1922, when Handy organized Black Swan Recording Company (the first all-Negro record company) Henderson joined him as the house pianist. Before long, his chemistry studies forgotten, Fletcher Henderson cast his future with the field of music, where he remained until his death some 30 years later.

Black Swan records were aimed at the "race market"—the word "race" in this case implying the Negro race. Blues were the order of the day, along with other forms of jazz, and Handy's studio cut many such discs. The top recording artists under contract to the Black Swan label were Bessie Smith and Ethel Waters, the latter an extremely popular singer who was destined to become even more so in later years. Accompanied by Fletcher Henderson and a variety of other studio musicians, Miss Waters added her vocal embellishments to such Black Swan discs as "Georgia Blues," "That Da Da Strain," and "Sweet Georgia Brown".

In 1923, Handy decided to send Ethel Waters on the road to play personal appearances, with Henderson as her accompanist. Henderson, it is said, was asked by his parents to bring Miss Waters around for them to meet, so they would be certain that their son would be making the long tour in proper company. Needless to say, the singer passed muster, and Fletcher was permitted to make the tour.

Not long after the arduous trek began, Henderson, Waters and company ended up stranded and broke, somewhere in the Midwest, and the tour was abandoned.

Returning to New York, Fletcher again found work in the recording studios, assembling studio bands and occasionally "jobbing around" the city with "pickup" groups* of varying sizes.

One night in 1923, when Fletcher and one of his groups were out playing a job, someone whom he encountered during the evening told him that the Club Alabam was looking for an orchestra. At first, Henderson was reluctant to audition for the

---

*Groups especially assembled for one given job, but not comprising men who worked together as a unit, day in and day out.

21

A remarkably well-preserved photo of one of the earliest of the *Fletcher Henderson* orchestras, his 1924 group. (Photo courtesy of Harry Dial) *PERSONNEL:* KAISER MARSHALL, DRUMS; COLEMAN HAWKINS, BUSTER BAILEY, DON REDMAN, REEDS; CHARLES DIXON, BANJO; FLETCHER HENDERSON, LEADER/PIANIST; CHARLIE "BIG" GREEN, TROMBONE; HOWARD SCOTT, LOUIS ARMSTRONG AND ELMER CHAMBERS, TRUMPETS; BOB ESCUDERO, TUBA.

job, since he had no bass player that night and was, in fact, leading a smaller orchestra than usual. However, it took him only a short time to locate enough other men to augment the band to full strength, and the group wandered over to the club for the audition. As a result, Henderson and his group won a contract there, and, with their opening, Fletcher Henderson and his band became something more than a sound which emanated from a spring-wound phonograph; they became, instead, a flesh-and-blood orchestra.

There is no clear evidence that "Smack" Henderson, as he was nicknamed, was ever much of a disciplinarian and, unfortunately, he was even less of a businessman, with the result that both the musicianship of the orchestra and his business fortunes fluctuated violently through the years. Fletcher seldom insisted upon promptness, never overworked his crew, and often shrugged off breaches of decorum which would have angered many another bandleader. The results of such an attitude were occasionally cataclysmic.

There was the time when the orchestra, scheduled for a 10:30 a.m. recording session at Columbia records did not begin arriving until well past noon!

There are legions of stories—eyewitness accounts—about appearances by Henderson's band in which as few as half the men were actually playing, the others smoking, or idly thumbing through their music. And there were times too when some of the men imbibed a bit too much, occasionally one or more actually falling off the bandstand!

There are stories, too, of how Fletcher himself would sometimes be so caught up in the music, or the solos by his men, that he would become almost hypnotized by the sound, and simply quit playing piano to listen!

Such anecdotes suggest that Henderson's orchestra might have been musically inept and, indeed, even the recordings by the group (which cut many discs) do not do a great deal toward disproving such a conclusion.

Yet the men who were in Smack's band stoutly maintain that, unlike many other orchestras, Henderson's just never was done justice by recording engineers.

Quite certainly what the Henderson alumni say

is true; persons who heard the band—and even competing bandleaders of the time—agree that Fletcher was not only a pioneer leader of big bands, but the organizer of great orchestras, as well.

The roll call of former Henderson sidemen would seem to bear that out, for it reads almost like a listing of the greatest men in jazz; saxophonists Ben Webster, Don Redman, Coleman Hawkins, Buster Bailey, Chu Berry, Tommy Ladnier, Benny Carter* and Edgar Sampson all were with Henderson at one time or another. So were trombonists J. C. Higginbotham and Jimmy Harrison, and bassist John Kirby. So, too, were such trumpeters or cornetists as Louis Armstrong, Rex Stewart, Bobby Stark, Joe Thomas, and Roy Eldridge, and drummers Kaiser Marshall and Sid Catlett.

In the years beginning in 1921, Henderson's name appeared as featured artist on a score of different record labels—Black Swan, Paramount, Vocalion, Pathe, Puritan, Columbia, and Victor, among others. So if Henderson's music was never well recorded, it was at least often recorded, one discography listing nearly 250 different selections which Fletcher recorded in the ten-year period from 1921 to '31!

If Fletcher had been a more astute businessman, the chances are that he would have retired early in life, without the tragic end he met, for in addition to his income from phonograph recording sessions and personal appearances with the band, he was early discovered to be an excellent arranger, a fact which bandleaders Isham Jones, Tommy and Jimmy Dorsey, and many others were to use to their advantage.

But the truth is that Henderson was never able to discipline his money matters any more than he could his men and in later years an auto accident apparently made him less than ever aware of how best to conduct business affairs.

By 1934, when the white clarinetist Benny Goodman formed his own orchestra, Henderson was inactive as a leader, and so desperately in need of funds that he was happy to sell Goodman some of his finest arrangements—many, it is said, for as little as $35.00 apiece.

But if the payment for those first arrangements

*Carter also did considerable arranging for Henderson.

23

was minimal, the recognition it brought Henderson indirectly raised the market value of every arrangement he wrote thereafter, his fame spreading with every playing of "Sometimes I'm Happy," "Down South Camp Meetin'," "When Buddha Smiles," and "Wrapping it up," all of which were best sellers by the Benny Goodman band.

All of this was quite an accomplishment for the one-time chemistry student who, in 1927 had lost one of his own band's best arrangers, when Don Redman had quit to take over as director of McKinney's Cotton Pickers. It was quite a feat for a man who took up arranging, in part, to keep other bands from getting easy access to his orchestra's arrangements!

As the fame of his orchestrations grew, there came also enough income to permit Fletcher to organize a new band, which he did, in 1935, taking the new band into Roseland Ballroom, New York, for a break-in engagement.

By August, 1939, however, Fletcher was again inactive, and this time he joined Benny Goodman as a pianist with the clarinetist's band, but stayed only a few months—long enough, however, to record "Stealin' Apples," which Henderson arranged. He was also with the Goodman organization long enough to participate in Goodman's 1939 Carnegie Hall concert, where Henderson received an enthusiastic reception for his new arrangement of "Sunrise Serenade," then a hit tune.

Soon after that, illness prevented the ailing Henderson from any prolonged activity in music, although he occasionally attempted to lead a big band again, notably in the winter of 1942, when he made an appearance with his orchestra at Grand Terrace Ballroom, in Chicago on New Year's Eve, fronting an unusually good band and romping happily through his long-time theme song "Christopher Columbus," and such other selections as "St. Louis Blues" and "I Got it Bad and That Ain't Good." After that, in 1944 and '45, Fletcher appeared at the Club De Lisa, also in Chicago.

But in 1948 and '49, the wheel of life had spun full circle for Henderson: He was back on the road as an accompanist to Ethel Waters once more, following an interim period of doing arranging for Goodman.

Back in New York City in 1950, following another serious illness, Henderson rallied sufficiently to lead a sextet for a time, and to write the score for *The Jazz Train*, a show produced at Bop City, a New York bistro.

Then suddenly, during the Christmas holiday season of 1950, Henderson suffered a paralyzing stroke which kept him bedridden during the last two years of his life—a period so anti-climactic that when he passed away in December of 1952, he did so without ever realizing the real impact which he and his music had made upon the American public.

His arranging style, which involved the pitting of the reed section against the brasses in a "call-and-response" pattern, practically spelled out the shape of the entire swing era arranging technique.

How much of Fletcher's basic writing style was of his own invention, and how much stemmed, instead, from guidelines set by Don Redman when he was a member of Fletcher's band, is a question which probably never will be satisfactorily answered.

But judged on their own merits alone, Fletcher Henderson's arrangements have stood the tests imposed by the 35 years which have intervened since he first sat down and penned an orchestration of "Water Boy".

And the years have not found his skills wanting.

CHAPTER V
Charlie Cook Orchestras

Billy Butler remembers Charlie Cook, and he remembers him vividly. Butler was a member of Cook's Orchestra from 1926, (though that was quite a while after Cook started his band). Once with the band, however, he stayed with it until the very end.

"Cook was an excellent organist and pianist," Billy reminisced. "Charlie and I became bosom pals. He became like one of the family and, toward the end, when he suffered a stroke, he stayed at my house for one solid year.

"Gee, he was a wonderful man—and a tremendous arranger. When I joined him in Chicago, he already had an office in the State-Lake Building, and was doing all the overtures for important theatres, and a lot of orchestrations that were published widely.

"He had a doctorate from American Conservatory—one of the first Negroes to receive one. When he started his group in Chicago (that was after he had the Detroit group he called 'Cookie and his Ginger Snaps') he called the outfit 'Charlie Cook and his 14 Doctors of Syncopation'!"

Butler thinks Cook may have cut records with that group, but he isn't sure. What he does remember, though, is some of the men in that band: Freddie Keppard, William Dawson (later musical director at Tuskegee Institute) and the superb clarinetist, Jimmy Noone.

"When I joined Charlie," Butler recalled, "he was finishing up his engagement at the Dreamland Cafe, on the West Side, and he also was playing once a week at the Pier."

From there, Cook's orchestra moved into White City, at 63rd and Stony Island Avenue and, with that moment, became one of the best known of the Chicago bands, its name splashed across garish advertising posters on elevated trains, street cars—all over town.

During the years when Cook's orchestra was at its peak, it cut a large number of recordings for Gennett, OKeh, and Columbia Records, among them "The One I Love Belongs to Somebody Else," "Scissor Grinder Joe," "Love Found You for Me" and "So This is Venice."

A typical personnel listing for one of the sessions, that of July 10, 1926, reads: Freddie Keppard, Elwood Graham, cornets; William Dawson, trombone; Jimmie Noone, clarinet; Joe Poston, Clifford King, clarinets-alto saxes; Billy Butler, Jerome Pasquall, clarinets-tenors; Sterling Todd, piano; Johnny St. Cyr. banjo; Bill Newton, tuba; Andrew Hilaire, drums.

Since Cook's Orchestra restricted its activities mostly to the Midwest—primarily Chicago and Detroit—any national fame it achieved came almost exclusively from its phonograph discs, those fragile black recordings in which its musical history was cut by the point of a needle, as was the case with so many musical aggregations.

There were radio broadcasts, too, for those fortunate enough to hear them, carried principally by station WGN.

But in spite of the publicity and the income, both from recordings and engagements, Cook found that by 1930 the Wall Street Crash had thrown his star into decline.

Billy Butler closes the Charlie Cook story by saying, "By 1930, the group was out of its job at White City, and just wasn't working. We couldn't walk into another job, as we'd been accustomed to doing. So when Charlie got a call from dancer Bill Robinson, asking him to come to New York to do some arranging for the show Brown Bunnies, he took the job, hoping all the while that the band would once again find work."

But with the passage of another year, and the playing of only a few one-nighters, the group—then under the leadership of Butler—finally disbanded, the closing strain written when, during a job at a "marathon dance contest," all of the musical instruments were stolen.

Discouraged, no longer hopeful of regaining their former popularity, the men of the Charlie Cook orchestra shook each other's hands, and went their separate ways—Billy Butler to join Fats Waller and the Connie's Inn Orchestra in New York in 1931, and the other men to various places and jobs.

And with those goodbyes, "Cook's Dreamland Orchestra" became just a name, and a minor legend.

At White City, on 63rd and South Parkway, in the Chicago of the late 1920s, *DOC COOK AND HIS DOCTORS OF SYNCOPATION* are shown against one of the most colorful and ornate mosaic backdrops ever! (Photo courtesy of Duncan Schiedt) PERSONNEL: (L TO R): BILLY BUTLER, DON PASQUALL, JOE POSTON, STANLEY WILSON (BANJO), WYATT HUSTON (VIOLIN), STERLING TODD, ANDREW HILLAIRE, DOC COOK, WILLIAM NEWTON (TUBA), WILLIAM DAWSON, CHARLIE ALLEN, ELWOOD GRAHAM. (PHOTO TAKEN IN 1927)

Born in Louisville, Kentucky, September 3, 1891, *Charles L. Cooke* (he later dropped the final 'e' from his last name) began composing music when he was eight years old. He organized an eight-piece combo in Louisville when he was only 15. Soon after he turned 18, he and his parents moved to Detroit, where he played in Fred Stone's Orchestra and, later, in Ben Shook's band. As a "manager" with Shook (who had a contract to furnish all the orchestras for Riverview Park, Chicago) Cook got his first opportunity to lead a large band. (Portrait courtesy of W. H. Butler)

DOC COOK'S DREAMLAND ORCHESTRA, shown in their home town, Chicago, in 1924. Some of the best of the musicians of the Windy City are present in this band. (Photo courtesy of Elwood Graham) PERSONNEL (L TO R) BERT W. GREEN, FRED GARLAND, ANDY HILLAIRE, FREDDIE KEPPARD, ELWOOD GRAHAM, ZUTTY RENAUD, KENNETH ANDERSON, DON PASQUALL, JIMMIE NOONE, DOC COOK, JOE POSTON, ROBERT SHELBY, JOHNNY ST. CYR, CLIFFORD KING

Photos of *Duke Ellington* are so readily available that one can chronicle in photographs alone, the passage of the Ellington years. Here is how Duke appeared in the 1940s. (Photo by courtesy of Hershey Park Ballroom)

CHAPTER VI
Duke Ellington

Entire books have been written about Edward Kennedy Ellington, the butler's son who rose to the top of the dance-and-jazz-music world in the middle 1920s, and who has stayed there ever since.

Whole chapters have been given to the songs he has composed during that time—all the way from "Soda Fountain Rag" (his first) to his more recent "Such Sweet Thunder".

Jazz journals have run complete feature stories on just one individual sideman in Duke's band—Johnny Hodges, Louis Bellson, and Cootie Williams, to name a few, and the Duke's talented arranger Billy Strayhorn, as well.

All facets of Duke's life—his composing, arranging, his biography, even his very personality (a most easy-going one!) and habits, have been exploited by countless writers, in numerous ways.

To speak again of Ellington in this book seems almost akin to pushing a worn plow through a furrow that has just been turned a hundred times. Yet to omit the Duke from these pages would be to nullify the very title of this volume.

For the Duke is among the greatest of them all.

Born April 29, 1899, in Washington, D.C., an only child until he was 16, Edward Ellington led a childhood far removed from the squalor, the deprivation of many of his race, for his parents were mildly well-to-do.

A boyhood friend gave young Ellington the nickname "Duke," and the title stuck, though no one then suspected that this young Washingtonian, then eight years old (and vigorously avoiding his piano lessons) would ever acquire a royal sobriquet to help distinguish himself from all the "Counts" and "Kings" of a music world addicted to bestowing such titles on its honored ones.

Just when young Duke's interests changed from baseball to music isn't quite certain, for between those periods, he showed considerable penchant for art and, while he was taking regular music lessons from a teacher over at Dunbar High School, he also worked at drawing and, in fact, won a poster contest sponsored by the NAACP, before his graduation from Armstrong High, in June, 1917.

The period of Duke's high school years is important, too, because it was at this time that he began getting musical inspiration at Negro-neighborhood "rent parties," where he heard some of the great pianists of that World War I period, among them Jimmy Yancey and James P. Johnson. It is significant, too, because while working part-time dispensing sodas at an ice cream parlor with the unlikely name of the Poodle Dog Cafe, Ellington wrote his first composition.

In 1918, as the "War to make the world safe for Democracy" was drawing to its bloody close, Duke married Edna Thompson, a former schoolmate. A year later, their son Mercer was born.

While jobbing around Washington and other nearby cities with various bands, (he painted posters by day!) the Duke became convinced that music might well be a good full-time occupation.

In 1919, Ellington, already a regular member of a small group led by Elmer Snowden, discovered drummer Sonny Greer playing at the old Howard Theatre in Washington, and invited Greer to join them. Sonny not only did so, but stayed happily aboard the Ellington bandwagon for 31 years after that!

A telegram from New York bandleader Wilbur Sweatman took Ellington, Greer, Otto Hardwicke, Arthur Whetsol and banjoist Snowden to New York; the job, however, proved an unhappy and short-lived one.

That hiatus, though, led to a meeting with Fats Waller, and eventually (through Waller) to a long term job, starting in 1923, at a New York night club which came to be called the Kentucky Club

All the *Ellingtonians*—Duke at the microphone—1947. (Photo by courtesy of Francis Williams)

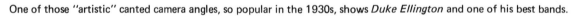

One of those "artistic" canted camera angles, so popular in the 1930s, shows *Duke Ellington* and one of his best bands.

during the 4½-year stint which Ellington and his colleagues played there.

One night the men in the band got into a disagreement, as a result of which Snowden left the band. At that point, the leadership fell to Duke Ellington.

Under Snowden's term as leader, the band had been anything but a jazz group. In fact, it is somewhat doubtful that it might ever have been otherwise, even under Ellington, except for the fact that a young jazz trombonist named Charlie Irvis happened along to join them, at which point the first distinct jazz voice was added to the Ellington sound.

The seeds of jazz had been planted, and they received, soon afterward, a fertile assist when, in late 1925, trumpet player James "Bubber" Miley was added to the band.

Miley was a pioneer—and possibly the originator—of a style of playing called the "growl technique." Muting almost all his solos, and frequently using a rubber plunger in combination with the growl style, Miley played a strong part in pushing the Ellington band ever closer to a pure jazz policy.

Trombonist Irvis stayed less than two years. When he left, in late 1926, to join the Charlie Johnson band, his replacement was Joe ("Tricky Sam") Nanton, a trombonist who echoed much, stylistically, of the Bubber Miley sound.

The additions of trumpeter Louis Metcalf, tenor saxophonist Rudy Jackson, alto-baritonist Harry Carney and tuba player Bass Edwards brought added strength to all three sections of the orchestra. At this point, jazz became somewhat of a mainstay at the Kentucky Club.

By now, Duke had been recording for some two years, their first discs, "Choo Choo" and "Rainy Nights" having been cut in New York in November, 1924. In 1926, though, the band's recorded output really began in earnest—an almost unbroken chain of phonograph discs which have now spanned some 40 years!

Between 1926 and 1929, the Ellington band moved into high gear, under the guidance of Irving Mills, an impresario who heard the band, liked it, and persuaded the Duke to let him assume its management.* Under Mills' hand, the orchestra started recording on better known labels than before. Furthermore, Mills got the band a long engagement at New York's famous old Cotton Club on Lenox Avenue, beginning late in 1927. In 1930, Ellington and his men took time out from their Cotton Club run to appear in the Amos 'n Andy film "Check and Double Check".

Now with saxophonist Johnny Hodges, who left the Chick Webb band in 1928 to join Duke, Ellington achieved international fame, thanks to concerts in England and frequent nationwide U.S. broadcasts from the Cotton Club.

And while the orchestra had cut literally hundreds of phonograph records since 1924, it was a 1930 disc of "Dreamy Blues" (later called "Mood Indigo") which gave the Ellingtonians their first big-selling record. Success such as this, added to the income from cutting discs under such other names as "Earl Jackson and his Musical Champions," "The Jungle Band," "The Traymore Orchestra" and "The Whoopee Makers" made Ellington's one of the most financially successful musical organizations of all time.

In 1930, Ellington and his first wife separated, the Duke's new love, a Mildred Dixon, a dancer whom he had met while playing at the Cotton Club. Son Mercer, and Duke's parents came to live with Ellington and Mildred—all of these events stirring little interest from the press. By this time, the Duke was world-famous, but it was his music, not his personal life of which the fans wanted to hear.**

And they did hear of his music: Through the fame of his recordings such as Strayhorn's "Take the 'A' Train," or favorites such as "Ring Dem Bells," "Chelsea Bridge" and "Johnny Come Lately."

In connection with "Take the 'A' Train," it is well to mention Billy Strayhorn, with whom Duke collaborated on this song, and several others, for theirs was a long, successful association, beginning in 1939, when Strayhorn—then an unknown—rapped on the backstage door of a Pittsburgh theatre, where Duke was appearing. Given audience with the Duke, Billy handed him the song "Something to Live for," a Strayhorn original. Recorded by the Ellingtonians, the song

*An arrangement which continued until 1939.

**Ellington's estrangement from Mildred in 1939, and his attachment for a third love, Bea Ellis, was scarcely noted in the press.

The passing years since his birth in 1899 have etched heavy circles under the eyes of *Duke Ellington,* but his stamina and creativity remain as impressive as ever. (Photo by courtesy of RCA Victor)

Johnny Hodges, alto saxophonist of amazingly sweet tone, a veteran star of countless big bands, from Bobby Sawyer's to Duke Ellington's.

A young-looking *Duke Ellington,* probably as he appeared in about 1930, the year in which he and his band appeared in the motion picture CHECK AND DOUBLE CHECK.

Duke Ellington congratulates fellow musician/bandleader Leon Abbey (left) upon Abbey's third six-month engagement at the Hotel Sutherland, Chicago. At right is Albert Logan, manager of the hotel. (Photo by courtesy of Leon Abbey)

An early and very popular photo of the *Duke,* mid-1930s.

became a hit, and led Duke to work with Strayhorn on other compositions and arrangements, too, for the Ellington band. Their association continued until Strayhorn's death May 31, 1967—28 years later!

Duke Ellington is remembered for his own compositions, too: "Sophisticated Lady," "I'm Beginning to See the Light," "Harlem Airshaft," "Cotton Tail," "Creole Rhapsody," "In a Sentimental Mood," and others.

And if anyone missed the first film in which Ellington and his men appeared, he had countless other chances to view them on the screen in such films as MURDER AT THE VANITIES, BELLE OF THE '90s," and SYMPHONY IN BLACK (all of them 1934 productions) and, later, THE HIT PARADE (1938) to name a few.

There have been official "Duke Ellington" weeks, concerts at Carnegie Hall, appearances at Newport Jazz Festivals, and almost endless lists of honors heaped upon this creative, unexcitable man of jazz, down through the nearly half a century since Edward Ellington mixed his first soda behind the tall marble counter at the Poodle Dog Cafe. There will be more honors to come. For though he is nearly seventy years old—well past the age when many musicians retire—the Duke shows little sign of slowing his pace.

And that, as far as a vast segment of the music-loving public is concerned, is exactly as it should be.

THE DUKE, and a "million dollar" contingent from his band: Ray Nance, Rex Stewart, "Tricky Sam" Nanton, Harry Carney, Johnny Hodges, Sonny Greer.

CHAPTER VII

McKinney's Cotton Pickers

Some time in 1922, Todd W. Rhodes*, a young pianist who had only recently completed musical studies at Springfield (Ohio) School of Music, and at Erie Conservatory, assembled his own 7-piece band, and christened it the "Synco Septet".

Springfield, where the group was born, is only 185 miles from Detroit—a short hop, even in that era, so it isn't surprising that some four years after the band was formed, it was booked into the Motor City's Arcadia Ballroom.

There, at the suggestion of the manager of the Arcadia, the Synco Orchestra changed its name to the Cotton Pickers, and expanded its personnel until it moved up into the category of a big band.

During this process, William McKinney, Kentucky-born drummer and manager of the orchestra was made nominal leader, and it was as "McKinney's Cotton Pickers" that the group moved into an engagement in the Greystone Ballroom in Detroit, in 1926. From that time until the day it died, the Cotton Pickers' name was inextricably linked with that of the Greystone—and with that entrepeneur of the ballroom, Jean Goldkette.

In the ensuing two years, the fame of McKinney's Cotton Pickers spread rapidly—so much so that in 1928 they landed a recording contract with Victor Records, which even then was a giant of the recording industry.

By now, Don Redman (who left Fletcher Henderson to join the McKinney's group in 1927) had become the musical director, with McKinney himself functioning simply as a road manager for the band which carried his name.

The richest musical period of the band's history now followed, for Redman brought to the group his arranging genius which had so sparked the Henderson orchestra. Moreover, Redman surrounded himself with some of the best sidemen

*Rhodes passed away in Flint, Michigan, in 1965.

of the time, and drilled them into a unique, showmanly Negro band which quickly became one of the top orchestras of the period—a fact which, in the light of the manner in which the public has forgotten the group, seems surprising today.

Bandleader Andy Kirk remembers the orchestra as pioneering some aspects of dance music. "Back in the 1920s," Kirk declares, "everything was based on triads and dominant seventh chords. Then some bands, McKinney's Cotton Pickers among them, added a sixth—an octave in a different voice. To get a full sound, they added a fourth sax, not doubling, but filling out the chord. I remember clearly that, when I first heard this change, it actually bothered my ear a little."

As early as July 11, 1928, Redman showed up with the orchestra at Victor recording studios in Chicago, even then bringing the basic lineup of four saxes—two altos, two tenors which, it should be remembered, became the basic saxophone section for most swing bands until well into the 1940s.

Those four saxophonists, Don Redman, Milton Senior, George Price and Prince Robinson arrived in company with two trumpeters, John Nesbitt and Langston Curl. Also with them were trombonist Claude Jones, pianist Todd Rhodes, banjoist Dave Wilborn, tuba player Ralph Escudero and drummer Cuba Austin—eleven men in all.

Victor recording engineers, having switched over to the new "electrical recording" process, which utilized microphones instead of a fibre acoustical horn, readied their preamplifiers and massive turntable, and then called for the first "take".

Redman and his men started out by cutting "Four or Five Times," and then followed with three additional sides, "Put it There," "Crying and Sighing," and "Milenberg Joys." The following day

The background is Greystone Ballroom, 1927. The band is *McKinney's Cotton Pickers.* One of the great ensemble sounds of the period, the band made the Greystone its headquarters—a logical fact since it was a Jean Goldkette unit, and the ballroom a Goldkette enterprise. (Photo by courtesy of Gus McClung) PERSONNEL: (L TO R) Todd Rhodes, piano; Dave Wilborn, banjo; UNIDENTIFIED SAXOPHONIST; Milton Senior, sax; Ralph Escudero, bass; John Nesbitt, trumpet/arranger; Cuba Austin, drums; George ("Fat Head") Thomas, sax/vocals; Gus McClung, trumpet; Claude Jones, trombone.

McKinney's Cotton Pickers, a photo taken some time in the summer of 1928. This orchestra ranked among the very finest of the many bands extant during the 1920s and early '30s. (PHOTO BY COURTESY OF FRANCIS WILLIAMS) PERSONNEL: (Standing, L TO R): CUBA AUSTIN, DRUMS; PRINCE ROBINSON, TENOR SAX; GEORGE "FAT HEAD" THOMAS, ALTO SAX/VOCALS; DON REDMAN, SAX-LEADER; DAVE WILBORN, BANJO/GUITAR; TODD RHODES, PIANO; BOB ESCUDERO, BASS-TUBA. (SEATED, L TO R): JOHN NESBITT, TRUMPET/ARRANGER; CLAUDE JONES, TROMBONE; MILTON SENIOR, ALTO SAX/CLARINET; LANGSTON CURL, TRUMPET.

the orchestra returned to the studio and cut five more sides, "Stop Kidding," "Cherry," "Nobody's Sweetheart," "Some Sweet Day," and "Shim-Me-Sha-Wabble".

From that time until 1933, the Cotton Pickers continued to "come in off the road" for occasional recording sessions for Victor, although all the subsequent sessions were held at Victor's studios in Camden, New Jersey, or at the main studio in New York's Lower East Side.

By late 1929, Redman had succeeded in expanding the trumpet section to three men and for recording sessions, would occasionally change personnel so as to feature one or more special "guest artists" who, in Redman's opinion, might serve to improve the overall recordings—Fats Waller the pianist being added for a 1929 recording session, as were Coleman Hawkins and Benny Carter.

To add to all the confusion about the many recordings made by McKinney's Cotton Pickers, there was at least one date, October 10, 1928, where the entire orchestra went over to the OKeh recording studio in New York and cut four sides under the pseudonym "The Chocolate Dandies," that session producing, among other selections, the band's first recorded version of "Star Dust".

Langston Curl, a trumpeter who joined the orchestra in 1929, and remained until 1931, recalls a number of outstanding qualities of the Cotton Pickers which made it a "musicians' band," particularly, he says, " . . those great arrangements by Redman and Nesbitt, not to mention the powerful swing which the band possessed".

The Cotton Pickers, which was one of the Jean Goldkette orchestras, continued to appear frequently at Goldkette's Greystone Ballroom, in Detroit, but also travelled widely and, along the way, learned its lessons well; it soon, in fact, surpassed in excellence the great Fletcher Henderson orchestra, especially since, at that time, Henderson was in a musical slump.

Redman, on the other hand, with his 4-voice reed section, was writing into his arrangements bravura passages which quickly became the envy of just about every other arranger in the country. Adding to the lustre of the band, one of its trumpeters, John Nesbitt, who was deeply affected by Bix Beiderbecke's work, and that of arranger Bill Challis, continued pouring still further great charts into the McKinney library.

The period of 1927 to '31, then, was the high point in the career of the Cotton Pickers—a quartet of golden years which ended abruptly when, in 1931, Redman suddenly announced that he was leaving the orchestra to assume the leadership of a band which had earlier been organized by Fletcher Henderson's brother Horace, but which now would be under Redman's name.

Once Redman left, McKinney's Cotton Pickers survived for a scant three years, disbanding in 1934. In 1935, Frank Williams, the ex-Ellington trumpeter, says he recalls having encountered, while on the road with the J. Frank Terry band, two large bands which claimed to have been organized from "splinters" of the earlier Cotton Pickers aggregations—one led by a Billy Bowen (who called his "The Original Cotton Pickers,") the other by Bill McKinney. Neither group survived for long, however, and McKinney himself ended up in Detroit, working as a hotel bellboy and, later, in an automobile plant there.

With the failures of those two bands, the meteoric trail of McKinney's Cotton Pickers sputtered ignominiously out, leaving only a stack of phonograph discs, nearly a third of a century old, to attest to the band's former greatness.

A pensive and solemn *ALPHONSO TRENT*, probably as he appeared in the mid-1920s — about the time when he and his band were playing their initial run at the Adolphus Hotel, Dallas. (Photo courtesy of Duncan Schiedt)

CHAPTER VIII

Alphonso Trent

America in the summer of 1905 was a nation living in awe of a group of startling young exposé writers known as "muckrakers". We were reading Upton Sinclair's THE JUNGLE, and standing open-mouthed at the sight of the new heavier-than-air machines built by the intrepid Wright Brothers, whose first plane had made its maiden flight at Kitty Hawk, N.C., less than two years earlier.

Theodore Roosevelt had already been our president for close to four years, and the boundaries of our nation were almost completely stabilized.

Chicago, New York, and other major cities were absorbing great influxes of immigrants. Our small towns, on the other hand, continued to remain just what they were, except as the dictates of births and deaths might capriciously decree.

Fort Smith—situated in western Arkansas, close to the Oklahoma line—was typical of such small towns of that time, a microcosm which could be easily observed by everyone who lived there. It was in this sleepy Ozark city where, on August 24, 1905, a son Alphonso Trent, was born to Mr. and Mrs. E. O. Trent, when Mr. Trent was principal of Lincoln High School.

Just about every town of that era had its beloved "professor," a long suffering individual who gave 25-cent music lessons to those of the town's children who could afford them—and free ones to many of those who couldn't. Back in Ft. Smith, little Al Trent could barely reach the keyboard of the piano at Professor W. O. Wiley's house when he started his first musical instruction there.

By the time he reached high school, Trent was proficient enough as a pianist to begin working professionally with the Quinn Band, out of Ft. Smith, which ranged over a wide area of the Ozarks in playing its dance jobs.

This was the age of fame for W. C. Handy. It was the heyday of Fletcher Henderson's earliest band—the one then accompanying Ethel Waters. Such entertainers as these were inspirations for many other Negro musical organizations all across the nation. But to many musical aspirants of the Ft. Smith area who'd never seen Henderson or Handy, pianist Sterling Todd and his Rose City band were inspiration enough, even though they were local. Trent drew inspiration from all three groups.

Following a short stint with the Quinn band, Al Trent, together with a cousin, Harry Jones, formed a small combo which included, initially Henry Smith, Homer Griffin and Brooks Mitchell. The new organization made its first appearance at the Basin Park Hotel, Eureka Springs, Arkansas.

As he worked in the small band and continued his high school studies, Trent met trumpeter Edwin Swayze, trombonist Leo ("Snub") Mosley, and alto saxophonist James Jeter (who later was to become co-leader of the Jeter-Pillars Band). Combining their talents with those of A. G. Godley, Eugene Crook and John Fielding, the group set out in 1923 for their initial engagement, a notable summer-long run at Stem Beach, Muskogee, Oklahoma.

Soon afterward, Trent undertook musical studies at Shorter College, Little Rock, during which time he carried on his profitable musical association with Mosley, Jeter, et al.

When Swayze left the band, his replacement was T. Holder (who was destined to form the 12-piece band which became Andy Kirk's Clouds of Joy).

A booking for Trent's group at a nearly-defunct dance pavilion near Dallas, Texas, brought hordes of new customers into the place, put the ballroom back on a paying basis, and drew the attention of the management of the famous Adolphus Hotel in downtown Dallas.

There followed in 1925-26 a year and a half contract for the Trent band at that hotel, at which time the group, now augmented to ten pieces, was calling itself "Trent's Adolphus Hotel Orchestra".

This record-breaking run of Trent's band represented a "first" in American dance music: the first Negro orchestra to be accorded an extended engagement in a top U. S. hostelry. That such success came to the band in the race-conscious Southwest makes their triumph all the more surprising!

During the band's early years, many outstanding sidemen were, at one time or another, numbered among its personnel, including Sy Oliver, Harry Edison, Peanuts Holland (1929-33) and Stuff Smith (1926-29).

Radio in 1925 was as novel a device, and a much more alluring one than color TV is today. On one pioneering radio station, WFAA, Dallas, Al Trent's Orchestra became one of the earliest bands to brave exposure on the new medium which many were still calling "wireless telephony".

Among the biggest pleasures of the citizenry of St. Louis in the 1920s—aside from their primitive battery radios—were the excursion boats operated by the well-known Streckfus Lines, romantic Mississippi River cruises aboard plush old sternwheelers alight with hundreds of pale, carbon-filament bulbs, and vibrating to the tempos of throbbing steam engines and syncopating jazz bands.

In the summer of 1927, the Al Trent Band started a spectacular season with Streckfus Lines by playing a "battle of the bands" against Floyd Campbell's band.

On the night of this historic band battle, the Trent and Campbell orchestras drew some 5000 persons to witness these two great Negro bands as they attempted to outplay one another, though unfortunately, the results of that battle are long since lost under the obscuring mantle of time.

What is known of Trent and his group in the five years following is that they cut a few recordings for Gennett Records of Richmond, Indiana (1927-31), among which were "Louder and Funnier," "Gilded Kisses," (both 1928), "After You've Gone," and "St. James Infirmary" (1930).* These recordings helped them achieve growing success in spite of the depression years in which they were operating.

Then suddenly in 1932, family matters forced Trent to quit the orchestra, by then truly a "big band" in terms of number of personnel—as a moment's glance at the 1932 photo reveals.

Unfortunately for the "big band era" which lay just around the corner, Trent in 1934, disbanded the big band, and contented himself in the mid-1930s with a sextet which included Charlie Christian and Alex Hill and, still later, with a quintet—the latter restricting its territory almost exclusively to the Northwest and the South.

Returning to semi-retirement in the town of his birth, Alphonso Trent passed away on October 14, 1959, at age 54, at which moment his orchestra joined in limbo the other great bands which helped popularize Negro big band sounds.

*Some recordings of the Trent Orchestra were also released on the Supertones label as "Duke Diggs and his Orchestra".

The year is 1932, the final one for Alphonso Trent as leader of his own big band—though the band is to carry on under his name long after Trent returns to his home in Fort Smith, Arkansas, and to working with a small combo. Anderson Lacy, violinist-vocalist, is listed as director of the band, Alexander Hill, the pianist in the group, the chief arranger. (One of the finest arrangers of the swing era, Hill also did arrangements for Claude Hopkins, Benny Carter, Andy Kirk and others. PERSONNEL: (L to R) FRONT ROW: JOHN FIELDING, BRENT SPARKS, GEORGE HUDSON, LEO ("SNUB") MOSLEY, HERBERT ("PEANUTS") HOLLAND, ALPHONSO E. TRENT. BACK ROW: CHESTER CLARKE, APPIE JACKSON, HAYES PILLARS, A.G. GODLEY, JAMES JETER, EUGENE CROOK. (Photo Courtesy of Mrs. Alphonso Trent)

ALPHONSO TRENT'S ORCHESTRA

Lovely *Lena Horne,* as she appeared in the Twentieth Century-Fox motion picture "Stormy Weather," released in 1943. Nearly ten years earlier, in 1936, she had been a vocalist with the Noble Sissle "International Orchestra" when it made such recordings as "I Take to You." (Photo courtesy 20th Century-Fox)

CHAPTER IX
Noble Sissle

On Saint Nicholas Avenue, in the heart of Harlem, lives one of the first Negro bandleaders to cut a commercial phonograph disc—his name: Noble Sissle. Born in Indianapolis, Indiana, August 10, 1889, he is now nearing 80 years of age, but nonetheless is still musically active.

Sissle's musical career began while he was earning his way through Butler University, working as a waiter at the Severin Hotel in his home town, and playing dance jobs with a small band which he organized for college and school dances.

Just before the Christmas season of 1914, the manager of the Severin made a trip to New York. While there, he heard a number of Negro bands which at that time were beginning to gain the attention of white audiences in the East. As he observed the enthusiasm of those crowds, he conceived the idea of getting someone to assemble such an orchestra for his own hotel. Further, he recalled that there was, in his very establishment, a young waiter who, he thought, might possess the musical acumen necessary to organize such a group for the Severin's ballroom.

Upon his return to Indianapolis, the manager discovered that the waiter—Noble Sissle—did indeed have an excellent background for the venture: Piano, violin, and voice training since the time he was seven years old and, still later, professional experience on both the Chautauqua and Lyceum circuits.*

Thus convinced of Sissle's ability, the manager called the young musician into conference, and commissioned him to organize a Negro big band—one which would be, coincidentally, the first colored orchestra ever to play a hotel in that city.

In 1915, Noble Sissle and his orchestra, 12 men in number, opened triumphantly at the ballroom

on the rooftop of the Severin—a band which included Russell Smith as pianist and Frank Brown as drummer.

After an extended run at the Indianapolis hostelry, Sissle and his men moved eastward, to a job in Baltimore. Soon afterward, in 1916, the band cut its initial phonograph record, "Little Bit of Honey," for Pathe, marking about the first time that a Negro orchestra was invited to record commercially.*

While in Baltimore, Sissle met Eubie Blake, a talented ragtime pianist who was later to write "Memories of You," and other hit songs. The two men teamed up, Blake as composer, Sissle as lyricist. Together, they wrote "I'm Just Wild About Harry," "Love Will Find a Way" and the hit Broadway show SHUFFLE ALONG (first presented in 1921).

As all this was occurring, events in another part of the world were taking place which in time would alter Sissle's life: June 28, 1914, Archduke Francis Ferdinand was assassinated in Sarajevo, Bosnia, thus igniting the fires of World War I. On April 6, 1917, the Congress of the United States declared war on Germany and the Central Powers.

Along the streets of every American city, there appeared a new kind of poster, depicting a stern-visaged Uncle Sam, face on, pointing a sharp finger and commanding "I Need You!" His command was not to go unheeded.

In New York City, Lieutenant James Reese Europe was leading a huge, Negro marching band. It started out in company with the 15th New York Infantry Regiment, but ended up in France as part of the French Fourth Army. And slogging along in that outfit—replete with bandage-type puttees and

---

*Chautauqua was a travelling institution, named for the town of Chautauqua, New York, where it originated. Like the Lyceum, it flourished in the late 1800s and early 1900s, and provided "popularized education" combined with entertainment.

*In 1903 or '04, Wilbur Sweatman and a 6-piece Negro orchestra had cut a cylinder recording of "Maple Leaf Rag" for Metropolitan Music Store; however, since only a few of the Sweatman cylinders were ever issued, the honor of "first Negro band to cut a commercial phonograph recording" still seems to belong to Sissle.

45

Noble Sissle and his Orchestra, as they appeared while playing at the famed Sherman House, Chicago, during the time of the "Century of Progress Exhibition," 1933-4. (Photo courtesy of Demus Dean) PERSONNEL: (SEATED L to R): JACK CARTER, DRUMMER; WENDELL COREY, TRUMPET; NOBLE SISSLE, LEADER/VIOLIN; HARRY BROOKS, PIANO; RAMON USERA, CLARINET/SAX. (STANDING) CLARENCE BERETON, TRUMPET; OSCAR MADERA, SAX AND VIOLIN; EDDIE COLE (BROTHER OF THE LATE NAT "KING" COLE), BASS; BUSTER BAILEY, SAX AND CLARINET; HOWARD HILL, GUITAR; HARVEY BOONE, SAX/CLARINET; DEMUS DEAN, TRUMPET; CHESTER BURRILL, TROMBONE.

When a secretary to the manager of the famous Adolphus Hotel, Dallas, heard the fine young orchestra of Al Trent, the band was at Oakcliff Pavilion, in a suburb of Dallas. Enthusiastic about the band, the secretary suggested they audition for a job at the hotel. Trent and his men complied, and a long-term contract ensued. *(Photo courtesy of Mrs. E.M. Trent)* PERSONNEL: (L to R): A.G. GODLEY, WILLIAM HOLLOWAY, T. HOLDER, JOHN FIELDING, ALPHONSO TRENT (HOLDING ACCORDION), CHESTER CLARKE, BRENT SPARKS, LEO ("SNUB") MOSLEY, JAMES JETER, EUGENE CROOK.

shallow helmet was Noble Sissle!**

The way led finally to Paris and to victory in November, 1918—to the fulfillment of Woodrow Wilson's dream of "a world made safe for democracy". With that moment, Sissle returned to America, and to his partnership with Blake. He did not remain there long, however, and shortly afterward went back to the Continent. He settled first in London for a job in a music hall called "The Holburn Empire," where he teamed with an Englishman named Harry Revel.*

One night when the two were onstage, a French impresario paid a visit to the Holburn Empire, his ostensible purpose that of hearing the famous Jack Hylton Orchestra, a British band which followed Revel and Sissle on the bill.

What impressed the Frenchman most, however, was the nearly deafening applause which was accorded Sissle and his partner. So when he returned to Paris he took them along, instead of the Hylton band.

Paris of the period following World War I was swarming with Americans: Ernest Hemingway, Gertrude Stein and countless other expatriates whiled away their time in the night spots, cosmopolites all.

Among the Americans in the French capital at that time was the wealthy young composer Cole Porter, a Yale graduate who had seen Sissle's American band at Yale. Moreover, Porter knew the young bandleader, and encouraged him to start a new orchestra in Paris—one made up primarily of American Negroes already in that city.

The resulting band, which included Sidney Bechet and Tommy Ladnier, was an immediate hit in France, a fact which contributed immensely to the creation of a European appreciation of jazz as a cultural form, rather than a novelty.

But early in 1920, Sissle returned to New York, where he resumed his partnership with Eubie Blake and where, with Blake as pianist, he turned vocalist for a series of recordings which started as a simple duo, but gradually added additional instrumentation with each passing session. By 1921, the group had become a 6-piece combo known as "Noble Sissle and his Sizzling Syncopators". This group, or variations of it, continued recording under Sissle's name until 1925, when its leader returned to London, where he remained until 1930, recording a long series of discs in Great Britain and appearing once again in the music halls.

Coming back to New York the following year, Sissle continued calling his orchestra his "Sizzling Syncopators," although by now the band had somewhat of an international flavor, what with such men as Sidney Bechet and Tommy Ladnier (of his former European band) still with him.

In 1934, he switched his band's name to "Noble Sissle and his International Orchestra" for a noteworthy series of phonograph recording sessions on Decca records, many of which included Lena Horne as vocalist.

By this time, Sissle was firmly established as one of the top society bandleaders in the country, a man with an international reputation to add luster to his name.

However, as his "society band" label spread, the jazz elements in his orchestra grew less pronounced, in spite of which, in 1938, he was recording under the name "Noble Sissle's Swingsters," and backing up the name with such jazz and quasi-jazz arrangements as "Sweet Patootie," "Viper Mad," and "Blackstick".

Through the depression years of the 30s, and World War II, Sissle kept up the furious pace—society dances, hotel jobs, theatre dates—even a motion picture short subject for Warner Brothers, eventually capping his big band career with a run at Billy Rose's renowned Diamond Horseshoe, in New York, in 1952.

Surprisingly, Sissle has never really quit the music field, although serious illness recently forced him to suspend such activities for a time. His big orchestra, however, disbanded years ago, " . . . when World War II was over," Sissle explains, "and the one-nighters went out".

But should a Negro or a white society engagement call upon him for his services, Noble Sissle is there to perform, just as he did when he was the darling of the international set!

**Eubie Blake, in the meantime, remained in America, operating the booking office of James Reese Europe.
*The same Harry Revel who was to become famous, a part of the songwriting team of Gordon and Revel, a duo which wrote many tunes for Shirley Temple's early motion pictures.

47

Jimmy Rushing — born James Andrew Rushing, in Oklahoma City, August 26, 1903 — is probably the greatest of all living blues shouters, and possibly the greatest living male jazz vocalist. After serving apprenticeships with Walter Page's Blue Devils and with Bennie Moten, he joined Count Basie, in 1935, and stayed with Basie orchestra some fifteen years.

CHAPTER X
Count Basie

A musician with an uncomplicated personality, with more than 30 years in the spotlight and little or no mention among the gossip columnists is a rare creature. Yet such a man is the "Kid from Red Bank," William "Count" Basie.

Buoyant and ebullient still, Basie has never allowed his long years as a bandleader to dampen either his enthusiasm for life, or for the music he plays.

Since Basie is happily married, and a father, one might think the Count's personality, unlike his music, a trifle "square".

Such is not the case, as any of his musicians will be quick to point out. After work, he frequently "lives it up," partying with his musicians—the bandleader instinct disappearing completely, and Basie the souciant-gourmet emerging.

Ernie Wilkins, alto saxophonist and frequent arranger for the band, has spoken often of Basie's immense appetite. "Eat?", Wilkins asks. "The Count starts off breakfast with ham and eggs. Then a stack of pancakes, and finally a large T-bone, with lots of fried potatoes." And sometimes, on the band bus, Wilkins discloses, Basie brings along a paper bag crammed full of fried chicken, cakes and cookies, to appease an appetite that may suggest similar habits of a few other jazzmen—the late King Oliver and Fats Waller, to name a couple.

And if Basie's appetite for food is immense, his appetite for travel (or his tolerance to it, at least) is almost equal, for the Basie band, since its inception in 1936, has criss-crossed the nation, rolling up a mileage record which would make a travelling salesman seem like a stay-at-home. That Bill Basie is able both to eat well and to travel far are tributes to a man who earned his first success against powerful odds.

The backdrop for our earliest look into Basie's life is Kansas City, in the late 1920s, where the young pianist, far from his birthplace in Red Bank, New Jersey, suddenly found himself stranded and broke as a result of the breakup of the minstrel troupe with which he had been travelling. When the Gonzel White Show disbanded, Basie found a job at a silent movie house, the Eblon, in K.C.

Not long afterward, an opportunity presented itself for Basie to join Walter Page's Blue Devils, then one of the best of the Kansas City orchestras. As a result, Basie announced to the Eblon management his impending departure.

The Walter Page episode was a short-lived one; in 1929, Page's orchestra, like the Gonzel White Show before it, split up, and Basie again was unemployed.

But again the period of joblessness was short, for Basie soon found a job playing piano in the mighty Bennie Moten Orchestra of Kansas City, one of the finest bands of the era, featuring as it did, Harlan Leonard, Woodie Walder and Jack Washington on saxes; "Lips" Page, Ed Lewis and Booker Washington on trumpets; Thamon Hayes and Eddie Durham on trombones; Basie on piano, Leroy Berry on guitar, Walter Page on bass, and Willie McWashington on drums. The vocalist with the group was the great blues shouter Jimmy Rushing, later famous as "the original Mr. Five-by-Five."

Suddenly, in 1935, Bennie Moten passed away while undergoing a tonsillectomy, leaving the powerful Moten band to be taken over by Bennie's brother, Bus Moten.

With Bennie's death, Basie quit the group, forming a combo of younger musicians to play a job at the Reno Club. Shortly afterward, he was joined by Walter Page and Jack Washington.

Hearing of a sensational drummer named Jo Jones, Basie added him to his group, and then Buster Smith and Lester Young, as well.

In just a short time, Basie had augmented the

49

group even further, eventually ending up with a nine-piece aggregation—three rhythm, three reeds, three brass.

The Reno Club job included a nightly radio broadcast via the new Kansas City station WQXBY.

One night in 1936, music critic John Hammond (a well-to-do scion of the family which owned the Hammond Organ firm) heard Bill Basie and his band on radio. Hammond told Benny Goodman about the group, with the result that Hammond and Goodman came to K.C. and encouraged Basie to bring his orchestra to New York for an Eastern debut.

Before Basie and his men left their home base for the city which musicians were calling "The Big Apple," Basie enlarged the band, at Hammond's suggestion, to include three trombones (George Hunt, Dan Minor and Eddie Durham), plus Herschel Evans on tenor sax, and Buck Clayton on trumpet. Then—soon after the band arrived in New York—Basie heard guitarist Freddie Greene in a Greenwich Village club, and added him to the band, as well.

The augmented orchestra opened in 1936 at the original Roseland Ballroom, then at Broadway and 51st Street, where it met with a chilly public reception that was strongly reminiscent of the treatment which audiences at the Roosevelt Hotel had accorded Benny Goodman's great band, only slightly earlier.

Almost discouraged to the point of quitting, Basie remained on for a booking at the Famous Door, a hole-in-the-wall night spot on 52nd Street. There to his delight, Basie (already known as "Count") discovered an audience which thoroughly loved the manner in which the new orchestra swung the blues—a massive, swinging musical organization that sounded as one big voice, whether playing from written manuscript, or "riffing away" on "head arrangements".*

In his excellent book COUNT BASIE AND HIS ORCHESTRA, Raymond Horricks describes the sound of that early Basie outfit:

> ... blowing into the wave of attack. The overall sound of the band took on the compact strength of a single voice, mellowed by an inbred relaxation. The men were ... riffing in

*An unwritten arrangement for which musicans have either memorized their parts, or from previous playing have a good idea how they will play it.

unison as one man, gradually increasing the ensemble sound in intensity and volume to create an essay in climax with each and every number they played. Sections would often come together behind a soloist, picking up a simple blues riff and punching it out to form a strong cushion behind the improvised line, in this way urging on the soloist to greater inspirational heights.

These qualities emerged in even the earliest of the Basie band's recordings: "Honeysuckle Rose," "Pennies from Heaven," "Swingin' at the Daisy Chain," and "Roseland Shuffle," all of these cut by Decca in New York, January 22, 1937. Several of these have been reissued from time to time, along with such slightly later recordings as "John's Idea," "One O'Clock Jump," and "Moten Swing".

In connection with the latter number, there is an interesting anecdote concerning the origin of the tune. Bandleader Andy Kirk reports it in somewhat this way: The late Bennie Moten once commissioned his guitarist-trombonist Eddie Durham to write an arrangement of "You, You're Driving Me Crazy". Durham, however, apparently had little liking for the tune. When he brought in the chart for Moten's band to rehearse, the leader discovered that Durham had played a neat trick; he had started out to make such an arrangement, but ended up with something essentially new, though it was based on the chord structure of the earlier tune. Moten liked it, named it "Moten Stomp," and played it frequently. It was this same tune which Basie and other bands still play as "Moten Swing".

But to return to the Basie saga: From that initial success of the orchestra at the Famous Door (and those days when singer Billie Holiday was part of the group) and continuing right down to the present, Basie and his big orchestra have swung their way along* through several generations of dancers, through the "Bebop," "cool jazz," and "funky" eras—through rock 'n roll, as well.

And though rumors occasionally have it that Bill Basie may give it all up and retire soon, there is no measure of evidence to support it—not in the

*Except for one short period in the 1950s when Basie disbanded the big band and led a small combo.

"Lady Day" was the nickname of *Billie Holiday* who — after becoming a singer at 16 — found a brief place, at age 22, as a vocalist with the Count Basie Orchestra, in 1937. That same year, she quit Basie, reputedly after a quarrel involving jazz promoter John Hammond, whom Billie maintained had too great a hand in advising Basie. A wonderful blues singer with a highly distinctive style, she fell victim to narcotics, and died in 1959, at age 44.

COUNT BASIE AND HIS FAMOUS RHYTHM SECTION SET THE BEAT FOR ALL THE OTHER BASIE—ITES AS THE WATCHFUL EYE OF THE TELEVISION CAMERA STARES FIXEDLY DOWN *(PHOTO COURTESY OF GEORGE HAMID, JR., AND THE STEEL PIER)*

A study of a youthful *Count Basie* as he appeared, no doubt, at about the time when he and his orchestra first came to New York. (Photo by courtesy of Francis Williams)

band, its enthusiasm, or the crowds it is drawing as this book is being written.

For the Basie band, like the Count himself, appears timeless!

The simple, elliptical piano stylings of *Count Basie* have long been a trademark recognizable to all but the neophyte jazz enthusiast. (Photo by courtesy of Willard Alexander Agency)

Count Basie and his orchestra, (Photo courtesy of Willard Alexander Inc.)

A rare and previously unpublished picture of a young "Speed" Webb, taken in the halcyon era of Webb's great band, the Indiana musical group which challenged the mightiest white and Negro orchestras of the day—and frequently won! *(Photo Courtesy of S. Lawrence Webb)*

CHAPTER XI

Speed Webb And His Hollywood Blue Devils

Just about every American, whether he claims to know anything about dance music or not, has heard of Count Basie and Duke Ellington. If he professes a degree of knowledge on the subject, he may even be able to identify Jimmie Lunceford, Chick Webb and Erskine Hawkins.

But, alas, the only one who recognizes Speed Webb and his bands of the 1920s and '30s is that rare creature who is a real connoisseur of the whole colorful spectrum of Negro dance orchestras.

For even some of the former sidemen in Speed's outstanding band (Teddy Wilson, Vic Dickenson and Roy Eldridge, to name a few) are far better known than the friendly, talented singer-drummer who led them.

What makes this unhappy circumstance even more deplorable is the fact that S. Lawrence Webb deserves a better fate. His was one of the best of that whole host of fine orchestras of its day.

Speed Webb now lives in South Bend, Indiana—not far from the Hoosier town of Peru, where he was born July 18, 1911. He's a funeral director, relatively inactive in music for more than a quarter century.

Speed packed away his big book of arrangements when he was a scant 39 years old, and turned his back on the musical public which quickly forgot that his orchestra was so good that it was chosen for a featured role in the early sound movie "On with the Show," which starred Ethel Waters.

And except for a few enthusiastic collectors of scratchy old 78 r.p.m. shellac recordings, the public also forgot those once-new and shiny phonograph discs of "Low Speed," "Spider's Web," "Liza," "If It Ain't Love," "Trees," and "What Am I to Do?"—all of them once readily available at record shops of the 1930s, and any of them capable of spinning out a mechanical facsimile of Speed Webb and his great band.

And to the record collector with the avidity and the good luck to find any of these discs today, the recordings call back to momentary life the sounds of a spirited and interesting musical aggregation—vociferous proof that Speed Webb should not be forgotten.

* * * * * * * * *

On a warm spring day in April, 1926, Speed Webb's orchestra, then in existence for only three years, arrived at Richmond, Indiana, to cut their first recordings for the Gennett record label.

Gennett recordings, or most of them, at least, are valuable collectors' items nowadays, but in 1926 they were as common as the old-fashioned ribbon spirals of flypaper with which Americans so frequently adorned ceilings of porches and kitchens—and only slightly more expensive.

The studios to which Webb and his men were called for that first record session of his band occupied a decrepit frame warehouse which sprawled along a weed-grown section of railroad siding in the industrial section of town. Whenever one of the ponderous steam locomotives rumbled past with its seemingly interminable train of cars, all recording activity had to cease.

The warehouse, a former piano factory, was a catacomb of small recording "studios," wood panelled rooms, crudely acousticized in the hasty, hit-or-miss manner of the day.

Ushered into one of these, young Webb and his men stood by, each with his respective instrument, ready to play into the cavernous mouth of a huge fibre horn, its tapered neck disappearing into an engineering booth just behind a glass window.

As a recording engineer moved the musicians into positions which would give the vast acoustical horn the most advantageous pickup of sound*,

*In those days, if trumpets were too close to the pickup horn, the loudness of sound would cause the recording stylus to jump, thus spoiling the master disc.

Speed Webb stared about him at the strange surroundings.

These were the same studios, Webb knew, where many of the greatest popular artists of the day were busily cutting masters of discs which were bringing them fame and money.

Webb thought briefly of Bix Beiderbecke, Tommy Dorsey, Jelly Roll Morton, and Fess Williams, all of whom had previously impinged their music onto great wax discs, for this recording company, in these very studios. And now, Webb paused to think, he and his men were ready to join them in the growing catalog of Gennett artists.

It was a seemingly productive session. Between the periodic, noisy interruptions by passing C and O freight trains, Speed's orchestra cut four sides: "Florida Stomps," "Shake It and Break It," "You Better Keep Away from Me," and "It Must Be Love," after which the recording engineer dutifully logged on a card the personnel at the session: Nelson Douglas and Earl Thompson (trumpets); Barker Berry (trombone); George White, Harvey Scott, Ernest ("Mouse") Green and Leonard Gay (on saxes); Fitz Weston (piano); Bob Robinson (on banjo); Cliff Levi (tuba), and Webb on drums. Then the engineer entered the master numbers which Gennett would use to identify each "take" and selection, and the first session was over.

Throughout the months which followed, Webb and his sidemen spoke often of their first experience with cutting phonograph records. Occasionally they wandered into some record shop, looking for one of the discs. It was not until some time later that Webb and his musicians discovered that Gennett had elected not to release the four sides; all had been rejected because of flaws in the masters, improper placement of the instruments during the session—or for some other reason known only to Gennett officials.

Disappointed, the band continued its dizzying round of one-nighters—Indianapolis, South Bend, Chicago, and up into Michigan, too. A growing territory for the band, and growing recognition, as well.

Calling his organization "Speed Webb and his Hoosier Melody Lads," the young leader (who had talked his parents out of insisting that he pursue a career as a mortician) had already held a lucrative contract, in 1925, at Forest Amusement Park,

Toledo. That contract led them, soon after the ill-fated Gennett recording session, to an engagement in Buffalo, and later to Los Angeles, to an engagement at Pico Danceland. It was there that M-G-M discovered the promising young orchestra. Seven films for Webb and his musicians followed, culminating in 1929 with the Ethel Waters picture already mentioned.

But most of the Speed Webb orchestras up until then had been small groups—in reality mere "combos". And in 1928, even that last small group disbanded while still on the West Coast.

As the men drifted their separate ways, Webb made his way once again to his home state where, in the city of Fort Wayne, he soon encountered his former baritone saxophonist Leonard Gay, who had just formed a new orchestra. With Gay's blessing, Webb assumed leadership of the group, which was soon augmented to include 13 men, counting Webb.

That 1929 Speed Webb Orchestra was the finest unit the leader was ever to front: Leonard Gay, Ben "Smoke" Richardson and Chuck Wallace on saxes; Roy Eldridge, Reunald Jones and Steve Dunn on trumpets; Vic Dickenson and Gus Wilson on trombones; Teddy Wilson on piano; William Warfield on guitar, and Melvin Bowles on bass. Since Webb had never considered himself a more than passable drummer, he added Sam Scott on drums, and thus moved out in front of the organization, into the position of director.

What followed were days of almost unbelievable glory for the Speed Webb band, days when "Speed" (who had been so dubbed because of the fast ball he pitched as a child baseball star) saw his orchestra playing "battles of the bands" against such musical giants as Paul Whiteman, Alphonso Trent, Jimmie Lunceford and Mal Hallett.

Then something else happened: Sy Oliver joined the trumpet section, and not even the stock market crash of 1929 could dampen the enthusiasm of Speed and his boys. From there on, it appeared, everything would be uphill!

But the lure of other bands, of more pay, and better prospects kept pulling the great sidemen away from Speed; by 1931 most were gone, and the final chapter of the Speed Webb orchestra was being written.

The period which followed was an unhappy one, without movie contracts to sustain them, and with even the best Midwestern night spots paying "Speed Webb and his Blue Devils" only token salaries for long nights of work.

There followed a period of turmoil, from 1931 to 1933, in which Webb even fronted bands assembled by others—a chaotic time in which Speed, deserted by his regular personnel, was drifting along on reputation alone, still hoping for better days to come.

At last, in 1938, the constant problems in leading one band after another crashed down upon Webb.

"One night," he recalls vividly, "I suddenly concluded that it was about time for me to think about what my mother and father had told me. I fulfilled the commitments the band had made, and I finished the winter of 1938, using a lot of musicians from around Cincinnati. Then I put away my arrangements and I went to work in earnest to get a degree in anatomy and embalming."

In the nearly 30 years which have followed, Webb has seen his second career metamorphose into a profitable funeral home operation in South Bend. There is a move underway to draft him as a candidate for mayor of that city.

But all this success and security has never dimmed his memories of what he still calls "the good days"—the days when "Speed Webb and his Hollywood Blue Devils" on a poster meant unusually great jazz to a dancing public.

Nor have the memories of Speed's band ever grown dim in the hearts of the real aficionados of the great Negro bands!

The greatest of all the *Speed Webb* groups, these are the "Blue Devils," as they appeared in 1929. A fan of the band hand-stitched the orchestra's name, in mother-of-pearl, on a large banner which the orchestra unfurled at each job, like some proud battalion preparing to charge into battle! *(Photo courtesy of S. Lawrence Webb)* Personnel: Leonard Gay, Ben (Smoke) Richardson, Chuck Wallace, saxes; Roy Eldridge, Reunald Jones, Steve Dunn, trumpets; Viv Dickenson, Gus Wilson, trombones; Teddy Wilson, piano; Sam Scott, drums; William Warfield, guitar; Melvin Bowles, bass; Speed Webb, director.

Promotion and flashy advertising were essentials of the big band age. A 1929 poster, typical of the time. Gaudy, big, and steeped in handsome hyperbole, they "sold" the bands to a dancing America. *(Photo Courtesy of S. Lawrence Webb)*

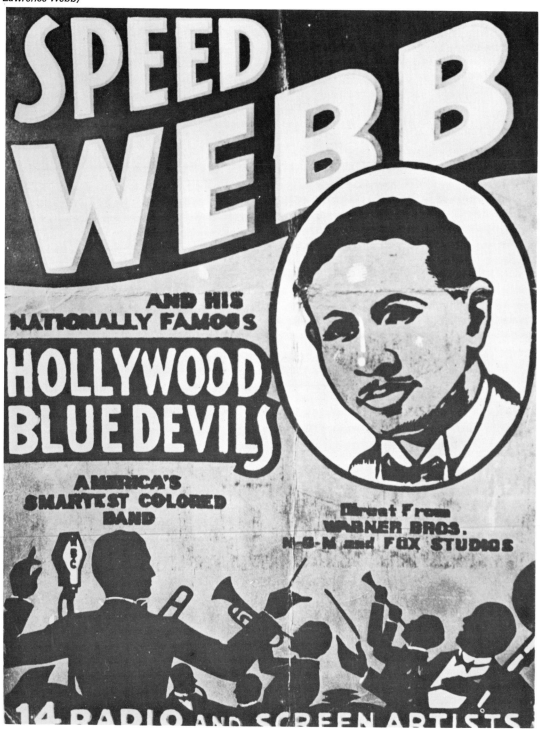

CHAPTER XII
Louis Armstrong And The Big Bands

It took a gunshot to set Louis Armstrong's musical career off and running.

That shot, fired on New Year's Day, 1913, came from the barrel of an ancient pistol, clutched in the frightened hands of Daniel Louis Armstrong, who stood there on that New Orleans street, never realizing what effect that playful, mischievous, childish act would have upon his world.

One result was that the small boy was arrested and sent to the Waifs' Home, a New Orleans reformatory.

A second and more important result was that while in the reformatory serving his indeterminate sentence, Louis Armstrong received his first musical training, his teacher a Peter Davis, who headed the Waifs' Home band. And because there was no important white man at hand to vouch for him, his mother or his stepfather, young Armstrong was not released from the reformatory until he was fourteen.

By then an accomplished cornetist, Armstrong soon obtained work as a musician in Matranga's, a New Orleans honky tonk. That led him, in 1915, to form his own band with drummer Joe Lindsey. The group lasted two years, almost up to the point in Louis' life where the jazz trombonist "Kid" Ory heard him and hired him to replace "King" Oliver, who departed Ory's group in 1918 to go to Chicago for a job with clarinetist Jimmy Noone.

The next year, Louis received still another offer, this one from Fate Marable, who was leading one of the foremost orchestras on the Mississippi riverboats. Louis accepted Marable's offer, left Ory, and joined the Marable band aboard the venerable sternwheeler S.S. Sidney.

Being a musician on the boats was not an easy life, but it proved a valuable education for the young cornetist. David Jones, who played mellophone in Marable's group, showed Armstrong a great deal about reading music—at least enough of the rudiments so that he could develop his repertoire without reliance upon memorization alone.

From that time until 1924, when he joined his first big band, Armstrong worked in cabarets and on the riverboats and, from 1922, with King Oliver's band in Chicago.

While there he received a telegram from Fletcher Henderson in New York, offering him a job with the Henderson orchestra, at that time (1924) not only one of the pioneering big bands in the nation, but one of the best as well. Armstrong's tenure with Henderson was a brief one. "After a year," Louis has reported, "the cats in Fletcher's band started goofing ... drinking ... didn't care ... so I went back to Chicago."

But during his stay with the Henderson band, Armstrong learned much which improved his ability to read music and, in return, contributed countless memorable solos.

The period from then until about 1929 was another one dominated by small-group activity for Armstrong—his own "Hot Five" and "Hot Seven" among them—although he was with Erskine Tate's 15-piece Vendome Theatre Orchestra in 1926* (during which time he switched to playing trumpet, instead of cornet). By and large, however, it was largely a period of small combos for Louis—which can be only touched upon here, since this is a volume primarily about big bands.

Armstrong returned to the big band format in about 1930, when he began recording activity in Los Angeles with bands which were not his own, but in reality those of Leon Heriford and Les Hite.

From then until he ceased his activity with big orchestras in about 1947, "The Louis Armstrong Band" actually was obe whose director was either Les Hite, Luis Russell or Joe Garland. Yet, with

*And, at the same time, with another big band led by Carroll Dickerson.

61

An early picture of "Pops" Armstrong in the 1920s, when the phonograph records by his "Hot Five," "Hot Seven," and big bands were giving other trumpeters the world over opportunities to play and replay Satchmo's solos, and then try to emulate them, if they thought they could!

The man who's known as "America's Goodwill Ambassador to the World" *Louis Armstrong,* shown here with his big band, (the Luis Russell Orchestra) in Boston, Massachusetts, probably about 1935. (Photo by courtesy of Duncan Schiedt) PERSONNEL: Louis Armstrong, Leader; Paul Barbarin, Drummer; George "Pops" Foster, Bassist; Luis Russell, Pianist/Director; Harry White, Jimmy Arshey, Trombonists; Leonard Davis, Gus Aiken, Louis Bacon, Trumpeters; Henry Jones, Charlie Holmes, Bingie Madison, Greeley Walton, Saxophonists. (Note: NOT ALL PERSONNEL LISTED HERE HAVE BEEN POSITIVELY IDENTIFIED; THEREFORE, THIS SHOULD BE REGARDED ONLY AS A PROBABLE PERSONNEL).

Armstrong fronting the group, it is little wonder that the public tacitly accepted such bands as being Armstrong's own. If they had been, however, it is quite probable that they would have maintained a more uniformly excellent musicianship than in many case they did.

Yet the big bands which paraded under Armstrong's flag were frequently creditable units, particularly the Luis Russell band, a fine group which was contemporary with that of Fletcher Henderson, and which often approached "Smack's" group in musical excellence.

While fronting such bands during the thirties, Armstrong influenced a whole school of new trumpeters, and a great many musicians on other instruments as well, in spite of the fact that there was an eighteen-month period in 1933-4 when Armstrong did no recording whatever.

An influential trumpeter, a superb showman, a unique vocalist, and a philosopher whose expressions are widely quoted, Armstrong does not emerge as an important figure among leaders of the Negro big bands. He does, however, deserve a place among those who helped to popularize the big band format among white and Negro audiences alike—in the process of which he added the fire and luster of his horn to such big band recordings as "Body and Soul," "Stardust," "Jeepers Creepers," "Ain't Misbehavin'," and "Dear Old Southland"— five valid reasons why Louis Armstrong has earned an honored place among great Negro dance bands.

Louis Armstrong, shown here at the age when he was actively fronting the big bands of Les Hite and others. Armstrong has enjoyed a long, mutually profitable association with the booking offices of agent Joe Glaser, for whom Armstrong began working in the 1920s, when Glaser was managing the Sunset Cafe, in Chicago. This rather unique publicity shot is, to say the least, a refreshing change from the prosaic "artist-with-his-instrument" type so common through the years.

CHAPTER XIII
Chick Webb And His Chicks

This is a love story.

Not in the usual sense, perhaps, but a love story, nonetheless.

For how else can you describe it when a music-loving public idolizes one man so much that when he dies of pneumonia at age 37, his funeral cortége is several city blocks long?

This is the sad, exciting, sentimental tale of one of the swing era's most beloved figures. the tragic man whose name was William "Chick" Webb.

Like many another Negro of his time, Webb was born into poverty. The place was Baltimore, Maryland. The date: February 10, 1902.

A normal child at birth, young Webb suffered an accidental fall during infancy which shattered several vertebrae, leaving him deformed and crippled—a frail little dwarf, destined to live a brief and painful life.

Less than four decades is pitifully little time in which to acquire fame, loyal friends, lasting devotion. But Chick Webb accomplished all this.

The year 1924 found young Webb in New York, a percussionist who had learned to play drums in order to exercise his nearly-paralyzed body, and who had become so proficient that he quickly found work with the small band led by Edward Dowell, in New York's Harlem area.

After only two years with Dowell's combo, Webb felt ready to try leading a band of his own, his 1926 group including such personnel as Johnny Hodges and Bobby Stark. The early Webb group, however, restricted its activities almost entirely to Harlem, not even cutting any records until 1931, a fact which seems a pity since those early Webb combos included Benny Carter and the great trombonist Jimmy Harrison.

As orchestras grew in size, Webb, too, augmented his band, drawing more and more top flight Harlem musicians to join "Chick Webb and his Chicks," as the group was then known.

One night in the mid-1930s, a 22 year-old trumpeter named Taft Jordan came to New York with the Doc Hyder band, a great orchestra out of Philadelphia. While there in Manhattan, Jordan wandered up Lenox Avenue to see some of the famous Harlem night clubs he'd been hearing about—particularly the Savoy, the Saratoga Club, and the Cotton Club.

"I heard music playing and I walked a little farther up, and there was a place called the Radium Club, where a seven-or eight-piece group led by Leon England was playing.

"I had my instrument under my arm and I walked on by the doorman. Then I walked up to the orchestra and asked to sit in.

"We started playing. Now I was—and am—a great admirer of Armstrong. They hit into a song and I started emulating Louis. I sang it through a megaphone, I remember, and played old 'Pop's' solos. too.

"The next night, at their invitation, I went back again. This time I saw some people in the audience who I knew by reputation, such as Chick Webb and Rex Stewart.

"Leon England had told them about me, do you see? Well, when I came off the stand, Rex introduced himself. So did Webb. Then Chick said, 'How'd you like to join my band?' I said yes, but that I'd have to give Doc Hyder two weeks' notice.

"Anyway, that's how I came to join Chick Webb and that great orchestra of his."

Jordan moved into the Webb group at the Savoy Ballroom in 1934, a band which included Reunald Jones, Pete Clark and John Trueheart.

That was not only a great orchestra, but it was led by a man who was one of the real gentlemen of his profession. And, somewhat more than incidentally, Webb was also one of the finest all-around percussionists of all time.

"Webb was a sweetheart," Jordan recalls, "a

really beautiful guy. If a sideman left him, even without notice, Chick would take him back whenever the guy needed work. That's how Webb was."

At about the same time that Taft Jordan climbed onto the Chick Webb bandwagon, so too did the superb saxophonist Edgar Sampson, who headed up a beautiful reed section, first of three, then of four saxes, but always embodying flawless intonation and attack. Then, too, Sampson took on a large number of the arranging chores and, in addition, found time to compose and arrange "Don't Be That Way," "Blue Lou," "Stompin' at the Savoy," and "Lullaby in Rhythm," in a remarkable association which lasted almost until Webb's death.

In 1934, Chick dropped into the Apollo Theatre near 125th Street in Harlem, to look in on an amateur show. There he saw and heard a singularly unattractive looking, yet somehow appealing girl singer, a 16 year-old orphan named Ella Fitzgerald. Webb saw in the young girl a truly great singing talent. And to demonstrate his faith in her, he coached her in singing, took her out of the orphanage, and hired her as a vocalist with his band. On June 12, 1935, Ella Fitzgerald cut her first recording with the Webb aggregation, a tune called "Love and Kisses," which almost immediately established her as a favorite female singer.

At that moment, Webb and his group saw themselves become nationally famous.

Although Chick's big band was one of the best-loved of all the orchestras to play the Savoy Ballroom, the men in the group had no idea of how strong a hold they had on the hearts of the Savoy patrons until one night in 1937, when they pitted themselves against the Benny Goodman Orchestra, then one of the reigning white bands in the world.

DOWNBEAT magazine reported the contest in their next issue, saying, "The Savoy Ballroom management was forced to call out the riot squad, fire department, reserves and mounted police to keep the crowd in check."

For hours that night, the two great orchestras alternated on the bandstands, each trying to capture the greater applause. In spite of Goodman's valiant attempt—in spite of his possession of superb Fletcher Henderson arrangements—despite the presence of men such as Ziggy Elman, Gene Krupa and Teddy Wilson in that impressive Goodman lineup, the contest went to Chick Webb and his Orchestra, without any question whatever. It was a defeat which Goodman could scarcely believe.

The fame which accrued after that placed more and more strain on the frail little drummer, as public and band bookers alike demanded constantly "The King of the Drums" and his orchestra.

In June of 1939, Webb announced, just after his band had played a one-nighter aboard an excursion boat on the Potomac, that he was "taking a few days off" for a medical checkup at Johns Hopkins, never knowing that he had already contracted pneumonia. He felt certain, he said, that this was a good time to visit the medical center, because the band would soon be heading out to the West Coast for a series of important dates.

"When we got to California," Jordan asserts, "Chick wanted to set 'em on their ears, and he wanted to be sure his health could stand the strain. He promised to rejoin us enroute, at Norfolk, Virginia.

"Kaiser Marshall filled in on drums during Chick's absence" Jordan recalls.

"When we got to Montgomery, Alabama, about five or six days later, I saw Ella crying. Then I saw the road manager; he was crying, too. The director of the band came over to the rest of us, and he said 'I think the man is dead'."

"We weren't thinking he meant our Chick Webb, and so we said, 'What man?,' and the director said he meant Chick Webb. He was dead. We couldn't believe it.

"Anyway, after that, we cancelled bookings, and we got onto the bus and started all the way back to Baltimore, on the saddest trip I ever made. June 16, 1939, it was.

"We went there, of course, for Chick's funeral, and there were hundreds of people there," Taft concludes, "lots of them I didn't recognize, there were so many. And all of them crying."

In that Baltimore cemetery, a stunned and reverent circle of musicians, family and friends paid farewell that summer day to the pitifully deformed gnome of a man who had loved his audience as he had his drums—with a passion that has far outlived the man himself.

The main entrance to "The World's Most Famous Ballroom," *The Savoy,* which opened March 6, 1926, under the ownership of the Galewski Brothers (they later shortened the last name to "Gale") and Harlem realtor Charlie Buchanan, the latter functioning as ballroom manager. Occupying the second floor of a brand new, block-long building on Lenox Avenue, between 140th and 141st streets, the Savoy proudly sported a 50 x 200-foot dance floor, two bandstands, and a disappearing stage. Fess Williams' band and the Charleston Bearcats were the two regular orchestras with which the Savoy opened its doors, with Fletcher Henderson's band as an added attraction during the first three nights.

The man whom many jazz enthusiasts consider to be the best all-around percussionist ever —*Chick Webb.* As a child, Chick worked as a newsboy to earn the money with which to buy his first set of drums, and reputedly sold three thousand newspapers in one day! (Photo courtesy of Francis Williams)

Chick Webb and his Orchestra, probably about 1934. Webb's long-time friend, John Trueheart, is the guitarist, Edgar Sampson the lead alto saxophonist. Sampson, who did much of the arranging for Webb's band, composed many of the top swing tunes of the '30s and '40s, including "Blue Lou," "If Dreams Come True," "Stompin' at the Savoy" and "Don't Be That Way." At the time that this photo was taken, tenor saxophonist Elmer Williams was not present, so vocalist Charlie Linton is seated in Williams' chair, just to make the band appear complete. (Photo by courtesy of Edgar Sampson) PERSONNEL: Mario Bauza, Taft Jordan, Reunald Jones, trumpets; Sandy Williams, trombone; Pete Clark and Edgar Sampson, alto saxes; Elmer Williams, tenor (represented in this photo by singer Charlie Linton); Chick Webb, drums; Joe Steele, piano; John Kirby, bass; John Trueheart, guitar.

Amid an eye-catching & spacious setting, CHICK WEBB AND HIS ORCHESTRA are caught by the camera during an actual performance, very probably during a theatre date. Originally called "Chick Webb and his Chicks," the band had long since dropped that novel title by the time this mid - 1930s photo was taken. (Photo courtesy of Hilton Jefferson) PERSONNEL: JOHN TRUEHART, GUITAR; TAFT JORDAN, BOBBY STARK, CARMAN MACEO, TRUMPETS; GEO. MATTHEWS, NAT STORY, SANDY WILLIAMS, TROMBONES. (FRONT ROW): TOMMY FULFORD, PIANO; BEVERLY PEER, BASS; CHICK WEBB, LEADER/DRUMMER; WAYMAN CARVER, HILTON JEFFERSON, GARVIN BUSHELL, TEDDY MC CRAE, SAXES; BARDO ALI, MASTER OF CEREMONIES.

CHAPTER XIV
Ella Fitzgerald And Her Orchestra

When the drummer-bandleader Chick Webb passed away, he left an orchestra and a library of music much too wonderful to be stilled so abruptly. Soon after his death, the band returned to the road, this time as "Ella Fitzgerald and her Orchestra," a group including many of Chick's former men, and retaining some of the drive and excitement of Webb's sound. Under its new name the aggregation was destined to carry on for some three years, until July, 1942.

There was a difference between the Webb and Fitzgerald bands, however; during Chick's lifetime, there was a rapport, a feeling of fraternity among the sidemen. After the drummer passed away, the group became more of a business enterprise. Men who had happily accepted $85-dollar-per-week salaries under Webb's leadership now wanted a hundred a week. Sidemen who had endured with little complaint, considerable hardships of travel and work when little Chick was there to lead them, now complained lustily about wartime inconveniences faced by the Ella Fitzgerald version of the group.

"We were coming back across the country during the war years," one former sideman recalls. "Tim Gale, a former agent then in service had charge of booking acts for the troops, was down in Biloxi, Mississippi then. Someone or other from Special Services sent hard-seated Army trucks up to New Orleans to pick up the band and take us down to Biloxi to play a benefit, and many of the men refused to go.

"That day, when those trucks arrived minus some of the valuable men he wanted, Gale grew rightfully peeved. The men who refused to ride in those trucks afforded those who ran the band a chance to make a discovery, namely, that just Ella and four musicians could earn almost as much money for bookers as the whole band was capable of doing.

"So it wasn't Ella's fault that the big band lasted only about three years after Chick passed on.

"Once there were fewer men in the band, the bosses didn't have all that dissension. They also didn't have sidemen complaining about wanting more money—even though such demands, in the light of the cost of living increases during wartime, were justified, of course.

"And there had been lots of other problems, too: For example, the booking office who handled us, it was rumored, was giving certain of its bandleaders bonuses to 'cool' the demands of the men for more money. Now that story kept persisting," the musician continued, "and that didn't help morale, although we trusted Eddie Barefield, who was the leader of Ella's band, and we knew he wouldn't go along with such a scheme. Still, it made us all mad to be working under such a setup, and it was another factor in the breakup."

All this added up to a quick end for the orchestra which, born of Chick's sweet personality and outstanding musicianship, had continued to exist because of the immense talent of Ella Fitzgerald who, in reality gave her name to a band she never really directed.

The music was great while it lasted, but the end was swift, and "Ella Fitzgerald and her Orchestra" are, today, long forgotten even by many who were there, and should remember.

In the world of the big bands, it seems, many memories flicker out almost as quickly as the musical notes themselves die away.

The Ella Fitzgerald Orchestra, on the bandstand at the Savoy Ballroom, April, 1942. (Photo by courtesy of Francis Williams)
PERSONNEL: Piano, Tommy Fulford; Guitar, Ulysses Livingstone; Bass, Beverly Peer; Drums, Bill Beason; Alto Saxes, Chauncey Haughton and Willard Brown; Tenor Sax, Elmer Williams; Tenor and Baritone Saxes, Lonnie Simmons; Trumpets, Taft Jordan, Irving "Mouse" Randolph, Dick Vance and Francis Williams; Trombones, "Rocks" McConnell, Buck Hardy, George Matthews; Clarinet/Musical Director, Eddie Barefield.

The trumpet section of *Ella's* finest band, November, 1941: Taft Jordan, "Mouse" Randolph, Dick Vance, Francis Williams. (Photo by courtesy of Francis Williams)

A rare portrait of young *Ella Fitzgerald,* made in 1939 by one of the perennially-popular dime-store automatic photo machines. This picture was taken at the time when Ella was appearing at the Southland in Boston with Chick Webb's brilliant orchestra. *(Photo by courtesy of Haywood Henry)*

Probably the finest female vocalist of the big band age, *Ella Fitzgerald,* shown here with tenor saxophonist *Illinois Jacquet,* whose horn has at one time or another livened the bands of Lionel Hampton, Cab Calloway and Count Basie, among others.

Ella and her big band, a group derived from the old Chick Webb Orch. (Photo courtesy of Duncan Schiedt) PERSONNEL: Bill Beason, Drums; Ella Fitzgerald; Elmer Williams, Tenor; Chauncey Haughton and Willard Brown, Alto Saxes; Lonnie Simmons, Tenor and Baritone Saxes. (Back row): Taft Jordan, Irving "Mouse" Randolph, Dick Vance and Francis Williams, Trumpets; "Rocks" McConnell, Buck Hardy, George Matthews, Trombones. (Not shown: Pianist Tommy Fulford, Guitarist Ulysses Livingstone, Bassist Beverly Peer.)

CHAPTER XV
Fats Waller

Of all the important figures who were prominent in the so-called "swing era," Fats Waller was one of the few who could manage to retain a small combo for recording dates, and yet assemble a creditable big band for jobs on the road—which certainly gave Waller a marked economic advantage over many of his contemporaries.

Born Thomas Waller in New York City, May 21, 1904, his father a Baptist Church deacon, young Waller spurned his parents' pleas that he pursue a career in the clergy and, instead became a professional pianist by the time he was fifteen.

After working as an accompanist to blues singers such as Bessie Smith, Waller cut a few player piano rolls, and some records, and worked briefly with the big band of Erskine Tate, in Chicago, in 1925.

Gravitating to Cincinnati soon after that, Waller, already a song writer of considerable repute, combined his talents with those of singer Una Mae Carlisle for a long series of broadcasts on station WLW.*

In 1934, Waller began recording for Victor, using six-piece combos which often included Gene Sedric on clarinet and tenor, and the Harlem drummer, Harry Dial.

"About 1935," Dial recalls, "Fats assembled a big band—10 pieces—because CBS wanted to book such a group.

"At this time, Charlie Turner, whom we called 'Fat Man,' had lost his job with his big band over at the Arcadia Ballroom in New York—at 53rd and Broadway. He was trying to hold his band together and, luckily for Turner, one of the musicians in his band, trumpeter Herman Autrey, had cut a lot of records with Waller's six-piece group. Fats must have figured that if Autrey were typical of all the

men in Turner's band, it must be a good orchestra, so he drew heavily upon that band for personnel.

"I suggested Joe Thomas on trumpet, and George James on first alto," Dial continues. "Fat Man Turner came in on bass and, in turn, named his trombonist Fred Robinson and saxophonist Al Washington, among others. Alex Hill did many of the arrangements for Fats' band, as I remember.

"We didn't do much recording with the big outfit, but I think Waller continued to lead big bands off and on, right up until the time he died* (I was with it for only about 10 weeks). When he passed away, the big band was just sort of sitting around New York. Fats, at the time of his death, was returning from Hollywood, where he had just completed a feature film with Lena Horne. He died on the train."

Waller was a superb pianist, whose giant "stride style" of playing, and his impish vocals could polish the tritest Tin Pan Alley tune into a colorful little gem.

An enormous man with a lusty appetite, an infectious smile and a love of life which seemed to affect all who surrounded him, he was completely original in his approach to music.

Before he died at age 39, Fats Waller had crammed a mammoth amount of living into his years, and he bequeathed to the musical world a prodigious stack of delightful and timeless recordings, as well as many Waller compositions including "Ain't Misbehavin'," "Honeysuckle Rose," and "Squeeze Me."

His big orchestra cut but few recordings, however, and for that reason his eight-year tenure with large musical groups remains, to this day, a little-known aspect of this talented man's versatile musical career.

*In 1933, while he was with WLW, Waller went on the road with Clarence Paige's Royal Syncos, and toured with it under his name.

*See the 1941 photo of Fats Waller and his big band for the personnel of that period.

When the irrepressible *Fats Waller* wasn't facing jail for nonpayment of alimony (a frequent event in his life) he earned a great deal of money as a pianist, songwriter, screen actor and bandleader—though he seldom was able to hang onto much of what he earned!

A production still of Lena Horne and Fats Waller, taken during the filming of the 20th Century-Fox picture "Stormy Weather." By the time this film was made, in 1943, Miss Horne had achieved star status — quite an accomplishment for a singer who, less than 10 years earlier, was a Cotton Club Chorus Girl! *(Photo courtesy of 20th Century - Fox)*

Fats Waller's Big Band, May 21, 1940, on tour. (Photo courtesy of Francis Williams)
PERSONNEL: (USUAL ORDER) Alton Moore, Trombone; Bobby Driver, Band Boy; Eugene
P. Cedric, Tenor Sax; Don Donaldson, Extra Pianist; Jimmie Powell, Alto Sax; George Wilson,
Trombone; Cedric Wallace, Bass; Slick Jones, Drums; Francis Williams, Trumpet; Fats Waller,
Leader/Pianist; Johnnie ''Bugs'' Hamilton, Trumpet; Freddie Skerritt, Tenor Sax; Bob Williams,
Trumpet; Franz Jackson, Tenor Sax; Dave McRae, Alto Sax; John Smith, Guitar.

CHAPTER XVI

Andy Kirk And His Clouds Of Joy

Andy Kirk isn't sure whether he was born in Cincinnati, Ohio, or just across the river from that city, in Newport, Kentucky; there were no official birth records kept then.

The date of Andrew Dewey Kirk's birth is duly entered in the old family Bible, however: May 28, 1898.

When Andy was still wearing knee pants, and the ankle-high black shoes then in vogue, he and his family moved to Denver, Colorado, where he studied tuba under the tutelage of an aged German. At the same time, he sang in a school chorus which was under the guidance, though not the direct direction, of Paul Whiteman's father, Wilberforce Whiteman, then supervisor of music in the Denver School System.

A job with a Denver band led by George Morrison served as Andy's apprenticeship in professional music. It also gave him occasional opportunities to lead a band, since Morrison sometimes had more jobs than one band could handle, and would assemble a second one for Kirk—or his friend Jimmie Lunceford—to front.

In the late 1920s, Kirk left Denver to go on the road with the George Morrison band, and ultimately to cut phonograph records with Morrison's group. Returning to Denver after the tour, Kirk worked for a time as a mail carrier, got married, and soon secured a job playing tuba with the T. Holder Orchestra.

Not long after Andy joined them, Holder became embroiled in personal problems which necessitated his returning home, leaving the orchestra permanently. Thus it was that the Holder band* passed into Kirk's hands, and was re-christened "Andy Kirk and his Clouds of Joy."

The year was 1929, and the big band movement was just gaining favor.

*Excepting four of the men, including Andy's friend "Fat's" Wall (not Waller) who formed another group.

At Crystal City, Tulsa, Oklahoma, Andy encountered an old friend and fellow bandleader, George E. Lee, whose orchestra was to follow Kirk's at the Tulsa dance hall. Lee told Kirk that there would soon be a job open at Playmore Ballroom in Kansas City. Would Kirk be interested in that job, Lee wanted to know. Eager for an opportunity to get in K.C. with his new band, Kirk telephoned the Playmore. A short time later, a representative of the ballroom showed up in Tulsa, heard the Clouds of Joy, liked them, and signed them up for the summer of 1929.

That fall, Jack Kapp, then an executive of Vocalion and Brunswick recording company, came into K.C. with a portable recording setup and cut the first discs ever made by Andy and his group.

"Kapp had heard about the Kansas City bands," Andy recalls. "There were a number of them, and Kapp recorded about five bands that time, as I remember: George E. Lee, Walter Page and the Blue Devils, and a couple others. The Blue Devils, of course, was an Oklahoma City band. Anyway, that was about October, 1929."

Kirk's first sides included "Mesa Stomp," "Corky Stomp," "Blues Clarinet Stomp," (stomps were selling well then), "Casey Jones Special" and "Froggie Bottom," all of which featured a teen-age pianist named Mary Lou Williams.

"In January, 1930," Andy continues, "on the recommendation of my friend Fletcher Henderson, we obtained a job at Roseland Ballroom, out in New York City. We arrived there at just about the time that the alto saxophonist Glen Gray was taking over as leader of the Casa Loma Orchestra. For some reason, the previous Casa Loma leader offered to sell me some of the band's arrangements and, since they were his property, it was okay for him to do so. I remember that I bought forty. Mary Lou analyzed them, and used them to study about voicing, and so on. As you know, she became a really great little arranger."

Some time between 1930 and 1931, Kirk encountered an agent in New York who was booking a great many college dates and some of the best ballrooms in New York and Pennsylvania. The agent began booking Kirk and his men into a tiring grind of one-nighters throughout that region.

One night, when the long, weary round had grown particularly unnerving, the dance circuit took the band into the Pearl Theatre, Philadelphia, for a week's run.

"The manager thought we had an outstanding orchestra," Kirk relates, "and he hired us as a pit band for the theatre.

"We stayed on there for quite a while, and played shows for Ethel Waters, Bill 'Bojangles' Robinson (what a tap dancer he was!) and a lot of other top entertainers."

The trouble was that while pit band work in 1931 meant steady employment at a time when such work was hard to get, it also meant that a fickle public outside of Philadelphia was given too great an opportunity to forget all about how exciting and wonderful were the Clouds of Joy.

So when Winwood Beach, near Kansas City, sought out Kirk at Philadelphia with an offer of work, Andy and his men completed one more show job at the theatre and returned to K.C. for the entire summer of 1931.

With the coming of autumn and the closing of the beach, Andy and the orchestra picked up a 16 weeks' run at the Savoy Ballroom, "The Home of Happy Feet," up in New York's Harlem area.

From there, one-nighters and short runs again followed, but with one important difference: By now the Great Depression had begun to curtail opportunities for orchestras, both white and colored.

There seemed to be no depression out in Kansas City, however, at least where musicians were concerned. So the Kirk aggregation scuttled back to the territory then presided over by "Boss" Prendergast and his gigantic political machine. There the Clouds of Joy found haven—and employment—at the El Torean Ballroom and at Fairyland Park, in 1932.

Kansas City, with its wide open atmosphere, had the effect on musicians of making them forget the nation's sorry economic condition. Soon Andy and his men had partaken of K.C.'s "lotus" and forgotten how cruel the country's economic picture really was.

But if the men in the orchestra had forgotten that a quick group of one-nighters down through Arkansas and Oklahoma served to quickly remind them.

For this was 1932. The pit. The bottom!
Banks everywhere were closing.

Kirk and his men had a little "gold money" when they left K.C., but they spent almost all of it in Little Rock while they were playing a series of shows there for a theatre chain.

Even as President Herbert Hoover strove valiantly to find the causes of the economic spin which the campaigning Franklin D. Roosevelt thought he could end, theatres emptied of patrons, and then cancelled bookings—Kirk's employer among them.

With the few dollars remaining to them, Andy and his orchestra made their way to Memphis, where they hoped Fair Park might give them some work.

Fortunately, they couldn't have arrived there at a better moment: The night that Kirk reached the park, Joe Sanders ("The Ole Left-Hander," as he was billed) was completing a run with his orchestra. The Clouds of Joy moved in to replace them.

It was a measure of good fortune which may well have saved the Andy Kirk orchestra from disbanding.

The Memphis booking provided Kirk with funds enough to get back to Kansas City once more, where they found awaiting them a choice job at Vanity Fair, an exclusive night club on Walnut Street.

Unlike other places in the nation, K.C. suffered little from the depression; consequently, many of the best musicians in the country migrated there—a time when Andy Kirk's entourage included such outstanding musicians as Paul and Ben Webster, and Irving Randolph.

Over on Vine Street, a singer-dancer named Pha (pronounced "Fay") Terrell was managing a night club, and acting as the club's vocalist, as well. Andy heard him, liked Terrell's "way with a ballad," and made a mental note to try to hire the

78

young man. Not long afterward, Kirk's incumbent vocalist Billy Massey did, indeed, leave.

So one night in 1933, Terrell joined Kirk on a short road tour which carried them to Denver and soon afterward to Oklahoma where, in 1933 and '34, the band found a job which provided them a nightly radio broadcast via a CBS network wire. These in turn were received by a vast audience throughout Texas, Louisiana, and other neighboring states, which helped immensely to promote the orchestra.

Late in 1934 or early in 1935, Fletcher Henderson came through the area, and he stopped off long enough to listen again to Kirk and his band. Ben Webster was with Kirk then, and sounded to Henderson like a perfect replacement for Coleman Hawkins, who had just quit Henderson to go to Europe on a tour.

"I sure would like to steal Webster from you," Fletcher reportedly told Kirk.

"What'll you give for Webster?," Kirk inquired jokingly, knowing all the time that the decision was really Webster's to make.

Henderson surprised Kirk by offering a trade: Lester Young, in exchange for Webster.

The truth was that Young's unique style was so distinctive that, in a large saxophone section, it sounded thin—a poor substitute, in Fletcher's estimation, for the big, gutty sound of Hawkins.

Within a year, Kirk was inclined to agree with Henderson, so when Young asked to leave Kirk for a job in Minnesota, Andy quickly acquiesced, and Young was on his way in 1935. Dick Wilson, whom Kirk had heard in Cincinnati, came into the band to replace Young, and remained there until his death in 1942.

"Oh those years of 1933 and '34," Kirk enthuses. "We were just so busy in night clubs that we didn't even have time to work our way into Chicago, and to the Brunswick-Vocalion studios to cut any records. So we didn't make any discs at all in that two-year period.

"But one night in 1935," Andy adds, "I wrote to Jack Kapp, whom I figured was still there, and I told him we'd like to do some recording again. The office wrote back, saying that Kapp was in New York.

"The reason, of course, was that Kapp had been to England and purchased the Decca label there."

Best of all, Kapp was looking for Andy Kirk and his orchestra. The result was that the Clouds of Joy went to New York that year and became some of the first artists to record on America's brand-new Decca label.

To help the band meet its expenses in getting to the Decca studios. the noted New York booker Joe Glaser obligingly obtained some lucrative bookings for Kirk, bookings which carried the band to the East Coast. Once there, they cut their first sides for Decca, including a sweet, new ballad called "Until the Real Thing Comes Along."

Their recording session completed, the band returned to the Midwest, and to another summer-long engagement at Fairyland Park. While there, events were keeping Kirk and his men so busy that they had no idea of how well their disc of "Until the Real Thing Comes Along" was doing for them outside of K.C. But then they got a one-night dance job in St. Louis, in 1935.

"I still didn't realize how I could get a booking on a Monday night," Andy muses. "and we sure didn't expect much of a crowd on such a poor night.

"But when we got there, we couldn't get onto the boat on which we were supposed to play—there were so many people on the wharf. I said to the men in the band, 'What the heck is this, anyway?'

"We finally got aboard, but not before the promoters of the dance found it necessary to turn away hundreds of people.

"The dance got underway," Andy continues, "and still I wasn't wise. Then somebody danced by and asked for 'Until the Real Thing Comes Along,' and that's what did it!

"Pha Terrell sang it, and when we finished, I thought they'd tear that boat apart, just by their applause. They screamed and screamed, and I suddenly realized what it was. And I knew, too, that the value of the band had jumped, just because of that one song."

From that night, the fortunes of Andy and his group improved rapidly. Bookings increased. The Savoy Ballroom called about the band. So did a large night club in Kansas City. Everyone, it seemed, wanted Andy Kirk and his Clouds of Joy, just because one hit record had sold so many copies—nearly a million, in fact, before the song's popularity began to wane.

The momentum given by that one great recording carried the band along for some 12 years then, although there were other hits which followed—"Little Joe From Chicago," "Walkin' and Swingin'," and others. The popularity of his orchestra was such, in fact, that it was not until the late 1940s that Kirk first realized that the big band era was ending.

"In 1941," Andy relates, "I met Nat 'King' Cole out in California, and we became good friends. He was just starting out then, but his popularity was increasing all the time. As I look back on it now, I guess we met at just about the time when maybe the big band was fading, and the vogue for little groups such as Nat's just beginning."

By 1947, Kirk says he saw the handwriting on the wall. Large orchestras no longer drew crowds as they should, and to make matters worse, an entertainment form called television was keeping more and more people at home.

"We went from Rocky Mount, North Carolina, to Ft. Worth, Texas, though," Andy relates, "and we had full houses at both places—and out in Denver, too.

"But even with such success, after I got done paying the musicans, and paying for the bus, I ended up owing the booking office $1700!

"That's when I said to my men, 'It's time to call it a day.'

"Other bands were folding, although Lunceford and a few others were still in there trying.

"I wrote to some booking agents then, and they all said something such as 'The ballroom where you used to play is a supermarket now.' The little promoters were quitting too, so I said, 'If there's no place to dance, how can people dance, even if they want to?'

"So in 1948, I came to New York and settled down at the Sugar Hill apartment which my wife and I had already been occupying for a lot of years—only now I got to sleep there every night, not just once in awhile."

Today, at 68, Andy Kirk looks back upon a career studded with such musical stars as June Richmond, Fats Navarro, Don Byas, "Lockjaw" Davis, Howard McGhee and Joe Williams.

With good musicians at his call, he still assembles his band for occasional dates in New York—dates which serve to help him re-live those moments when his Clouds of Joy swept pleasantly across America's most sunny musical scene.

An early "on stage" look at *Andy Kirk and his Clouds of Joy.* PERSONNEL: (USUAL ORDER) Crane Prince, TPT; Andy Kirk, Bass/Tuba; Harry Lawson, Trumpet; Claude Williams, Violin; Allen Durham, Trombone; Billy Massey, Vocalist; "Crack" MacNeal, Drums; Bill Dirvin, Banjo/Guitar; John O. Williams, Alto; Marion Jackson, Piano; Lawrence Freeman and John Harrington, saxes.

Agent Joe Glaser, though somewhat blunt and self-assertive, nonetheless maintained long associations with his various artists, all of whom swear by his talent as an agent, and his business acumen. *ANDY KIRK,* shown here in the early days of his long tenure with Glaser's office, which also included on its roster Louis Armstrong and Lionel Hampton.

ANDY KIRK'S NAME, on the marquee of the big Loew's State Theatre, in the center of Times Square — a long way upward from the modest Oklahoma dance spots where Andy and his men started their musical advance.

The original *Clouds of Joy,* as they appeared in 1929, soon after Andy Kirk assumed the leadership of the group, much of which earlier was the T. Holder Band. Kirk is one of the best-loved figures of the big band era. Personnel: (Standing) John Harrington, Clarinet/sax; "Crack" Mac Neal Drums; Allen Durham, Trombone; Harry "Big Jim" Lawson, trumpet; Jean Prince, trumpet; John O. Williams, Alto. (Seated): Marion Jackson, Piano; Billy Massey Vocals; Claude Williams, violin; Andy Kirk, Leader/Tuba/Bass; Bill Dirvin, Banjo/Guitar; Lawrence "Slim" Freeman, Tenor.

CHAPTER XVII

Erskine Hawkins

"The nucleus of the Erskine Hawkins orchestra," says saxophonist Haywood Henry, "was a group of boys from Tuggles Institute and Industrial High School in Birmingham, Alabama. Some of us had known each other since we were only five or six years old—a long time before President Trenholm, of Alabama State Teachers College, discovered the group of us, Erskine, Bob Range, Dud Bascomb and so on, and offered us those scholarships which brought us to college in 1930."

But discover them the college did, and those boys, mere teenagers at the time, became the 'Bama State Collegians, a dance orchestra which soon attracted widespread attention.

"Even while we were still in college," Henry discloses, "Joe Glaser the agent had already given us a nice play at the Grand Terrace Ballroom in Chicago.

"And then in 1935, the band got another break, a booking at the Harlem Opera House in New York City.

"It sounds very silly now," Henry continues, "but at that time, we got a dollar apiece when we got through playing a dance; the rest of the money went to the college. Since the school took care of our room and board, though, that dollar was pretty good, besides which the school later raised the amount to two dollars, just because the band was very popular.

"Now President Trenholm had told us that if we ever got a break, it was okay with him for us to leave. Well, a lot of bookers were after that band, and finally one of them took it over, leaving us with no official connection with the college. We had the instruments overhauled, and we returned them to the school, and were on our own.

"We dropped the name 'Bama State Collegians then," Henry recalls, "but we weren't really sure what to call the group because, as a matter of fact,

Erskine Hawkins didn't want to be leader. None of us wanted it! We had to darned near force Erskine to assume the leadership, which we felt sure was a good choice. He was talented, a showman, a fine trumpeter—with all those high notes of his. So we talked him into it."

By 1937, there was a change of agencies, with Moe Gale taking over the representation, and at that point the band really began to achieve success, with some 50 weeks of work per year. That same year, the band began cutting records.

Haywood Henry describes those first discs as "terrible," and recalls further that Dud Bascomb said, upon hearing the first ones, "How bad could we get?"

"We just didn't know how to record," says Henry. "We knew how to play in person, but on records, everyone in the sax section had a different vibrato. We weren't too much in tune, either."

By 1939, however, Erskine Hawkins and his orchestra had learned how to make recordings—good ones. Moreover, the band was then a thoroughly established attraction at the wonderful old Savoy Ballroom, which Haywood still remembers with considerable nostalgia.

"Why did I like the Savoy?," Henry says. "I guess it was the intimacy. You were very close to the people, and you knew everybody. Because the Savoy used two bands, you were off the stand 40 minutes an hour, so you were socializing with your friends, people who knew you by name.

"There's something else I like to remember: The competitive spirit of playing at the Savoy, and how the people there appreciated music at that time. It's funny to me now, the reaction of the public to music today, as compared to then."

Erskine Hawkins recalls pleasantly another aspect of the Savoy, a facet of its operation which led his orchestra straight to its first great hit record, in 1939.

In the days of "forty on and forty off" the bandstand at that ballroom, bands frequently used some sort of short musical break at the end of their intervals on the stand—each one a signal to the opposing band that it was time to change places. With the Hawkins band, that "chaser" was a short riff, a catchy and original thing created by Hawkins and his men for the express purpose of identifying the close of a set.

One day while in the Victor recording studio, Erskine Hawkins and his men, in need of one more tune to record, conceived the thought of hastily expanding their little "musical break" into a complete tune.* The resulting composition, recorded that day, was just as hastily titled "Tuxedo Junction," in honor of the corners at the end of the street car tracks in Birmingham, Alabama, where young Hawkins used to get off the trolley and walk two additional blocks to famed Tuxedo Park, and the wooden dance pavilion where, as a boy, he played trumpet.

"Tuxedo Junction" was a sensation, and was followed by a long series of great Hawkins recordings, among them "Cherry," "Tippin' In," "After Hours," and "Midnight Stroll," all parts of a huge library which also included sweet ballads such as "Whispering Grass" and "Leanin' on the Old Top Rail". Such diversity made the Hawkins band a truly formidable competitor for any other group with the courage to meet this band on its home ground, the Savoy Ballroom.

"I'll never forget that we played a battle of the bands," says Haywood Henry, "against an orchestra which really outplayed us. And, do you know, a couple of the guys in our band actually cried? It was Lionel Hampton's band that caused it, when he first came to New York in the 1940s, and had such men with him as Illinois Jacquet. After all," adds Henry, "we didn't expect them to be so good and, consequently, we didn't prepare for them.

"Not only that, but if we knew that the other band had a very famous arrangement, we would try to duplicate the chart, and play it better, if we could.

"Now we knew that Lionel was famous for 'Flying Home,' and he fooled us; he played

*The tune "Hold Tight," although developed by a different composer, is said to have evolved in much the same way.

something we thought was 'Flying Home,' and we went into our version. Then he came back with the real 'Flying Home,' and the house came down! We didn't know what to do. He'd beaten us at our game.

"Besides that, we had an ending on our version of that song, one in which we closed out with the theme from 'Rhapsody in Blue' and this was our BIG ending. Well, right at the crucial moment, our drummer's foot pedal broke, so instead of getting this big, big ending, absolutely nothing happened!

"We also played against Bunny Berigan," Henry reminisces, "and we knew about his playing with Tommy Dorsey's outfit. We also knew, or thought we knew, that Berigan had no band—no organized band, anyway.

"So, again, we didn't prepare. And guess what? Berigan brought a band of all stars—Georgie Auld, and Ray Conniff among them. They came up with those soloists, such as that fine drummer, Buddy Rich.

"Well, our drummer was a great swing percussionist, but he wasn't a soloist. He didn't care for solos.

"Buddy played a wonderful drum solo that night, and then we opened up with our drummer, who was supposed to take some solos to lead us in. He started beating rhythm and we were waiting for some drum breaks to throw us in, and that guy just didn't want to take a break. He kept saying to us, 'Jump in the best way you can . . . jump in the best way you can!' I'll never forget it!"

Then there was the night Erskine's band played against the mighty Duke.

"We stood on the platform and just appreciated it, believe me.

"Then the Duke played 'Roll out the Barrel' ('we'll have a barrel of fun') and announced that he'd had a 'barrel of fun' playing against us. He said, 'These young fellows sure made us work. Give them a big hand.' We all cherish that moment, and I'm not kidding."

It is strange how, once Erskine Hawkins and his men played at the Savoy Ballroom, their lives became so interwoven with the place that from then on, their fates seemed cast together—those of the dance hall and the Hawkins band.

For when the Savoy closed, in the late 1950s, so too did the Erskine Hawkins orchestra disband, the leader thereafter fronting small combos, with only an occasional one-nighter with a specially-assembled full orchestra in the years that have followed.

The Savoy—Erskine Hawkins—Tuxedo Junction—Alabama State Teachers College: Four very diverse elements. together, created an orchestra which became a rich part of dance band history!

ERSKINE HAWKINS AND HIS ORCHESTRA, a photo taken when the band was at the peak of its fame.

Bob Range, Erskine Hawkins' trombonist, a vital overtone in the mighty voice of the Hawkins orchestra. (Photo by courtesy of Haywood Henry)

One of the earliest known photos of "The Twentieth Century Gabriel," *Erskine Hawkins,* a picture taken during the days when he was just a sideman in the "Bama State Collegians," one of several dance orchestras sponsored by Alabama State Teachers College. (Photo by courtesy of Haywood Henry)

HAYWOOD HENRY went to work for Erskine Hawkins with the expectation of staying, he says, "for about two weeks." The actual length of the association: 23 years! (Photo courtesy Haywood Henry)

Another well known member of the Erskine Hawkins group, vocalist/saxophonist *Jimmie Mitchell.* (Photo by courtesy of Haywood Henry)

Suave and assured, *ERSKINE HAWKINS,* the man who had to be talked into being a bandleader is shown here in a rare photo, one taken of him WITHOUT his trumpet.

Here are *Andy Kirk and his Clouds of Joy* at Rainbow Ballroom, Buffalo, New York, about 1934 or '35. (Photo courtesy Andy Kirk) *PERSONNEL:* Mary Lou Williams, Piano; Ted Brinson, Guitar; Pha Terrell, Vocals; John Williams (Husband of Mary Lou), Alto; John Harrington, Alto/Clarinet; Dick Wilson, Tenor; Andy Kirk, Leader/Baritone; (Back Row) Booker Collins (called "Itty Bitty"), Bass; Ben Thigpen, Drums; Harry Lawson, (Next man unidentified, may be Gene Price), Earl Thompson, Trumpets; Theodore Donley, Trombone.

A candid look at *Don Redman,* who possessed so many musical talents that one of his nicknames was "The Octopus." Redman, a college graduate himself, fronted a band which included, simultaneously, six other college graduates and two other men with either two or three years of college work. All others were high school graduates, making Redman's one of the best-educated orchestras of all time. (Photo courtesy of Mrs. Don Redman)

CHAPTER XVIII
Don Redman

Among the greatest losses to American jazz in 1963 was that of Donald Matthew Redman, the brilliant arranger, composer, leader and saxophonist who went from his birthplace in the hills of West Virginia to fame, and a life of serene security in one of Harlem's most pleasant apartment buildings.

When the American Federation of Musicians paid final tribute to Redman, they reviewed his life in rapid, kaleidoscopic form: Born Piedmont, West Virginia, July 29, 1900; both parents musically talented, their child a musical genius who played trumpet at 3, joined a band when he was six and who, in childhood, studied every instrument and, in addition, harmony, theory and composition.

But behind the cold, factual recitation of Don Redman's early years there is the warm story of a quiet and intelligent young man who, armed with four years' education at Harper's Ferry College, and three years at Boston Conservatory, said goodbye to his mother and father and, with their blessing, left his father's band to try making his own way to success.

In 1924, just three years after his graduation from Boston Conservatory, Don Redman joined the great Fletcher Henderson Orchestra, then an 11-piece group which included Louis Armstrong, drummer Kaiser Marshall, and tenor saxophonist Coleman Hawkins.

As Redman sat in the 3-man saxophone section, his keen ear and amazing pitch told him that much which he was hearing could be improved, although Henderson's was one of the finest orchestras of its time.

And before Armstrong left Henderson in late 1925, Don Redman had caught not only the spirit with which "Pops" imbued every solo he played, but the young arranger felt capable of capturing in written arrangements much of the excitement and the pure jazz which poured from Armstrong's mighty cornet.

It is doubtful that anyone, other than Redman, could have done quite so much for the budding era of the big band. For Redman could play—besides saxophone and cornet—trombone. violin, piano, drums and bass, and could "hear" every instrument in his own mind, with the result that he needed no musical device at hand in order to write entire scores for the orchestra.

By October 21, 1925, when Armstrong cut his final recordings as a member of the Henderson organization, Redman had already begun to write scores for the band—the first musician to skillfully blend academic, formal training with true jazz. The easy-going Henderson, in his bumbling way, had nurtured into full flower a brilliant figure who was destined to leave his mark ineradicably upon every Fletcher Henderson band thereafter, and to set forth arranging devices which Fletcher himself would re-use long after Redman closed his little alto sax case following his last job with Henderson, in 1927.

In that same year, Redman assumed the position of director of McKinney's Cotton Pickers, a Midwestern orchestra which was already of more than ordinary merit when Don came along to help shape their destinies.

Under Redman's tutelage, McKinney's Cotton Pickers became one of the most popular big bands of the period, cutting such memorable discs as "Four of Five Times," "Cherry" (which Don composed), and "There's a Rainbow 'Round My Shoulder," not to mention "Save it, Pretty Mama," the latter featuring Don on the vocal, as had a number of Fletcher Henderson discs before it.

In mid-1931, Redman left the McKinney's orchestra and in October, 1932, appeared on the musical scene once again, this time with the first of his own orchestras, one formed earlier by Fletcher Henderson's brother Horace. The group's initial appearance was at Connie's Inn, in New York City, followed in 1933 by a pioneer radio series, sponsored by "Chipso" soap, and carried coast-to-coast by NBC—making it the first Negro band to be accorded a commercial broadcast.

While the fame of Redman's orchestra spread much too slowly, that of his skill as an arranger did not, with the result that the Dorsey brothers, Paul Whiteman, Vincent Lopez and Bobby Byrne commissioned the young Negro to write for their orchestras, too—as did other leaders.

On Brunswick recordings and, later, on Bluebird and Victor discs, Redman and his men transcribed "I Heard," "Milenberg Joys," "Sweet Leilani," "Gee, Baby, Ain't I Good to You?" and dozens of other hit tunes which added to the prestige of the orchestra.

Night after night, for about eight years, "Chant of the Weed"—the smokey and haunting theme of the orchestra, a Redman original—ushered in the band for dances and broadcasts; however, poor management and lack of public acceptance worked against the two bands which Redman led during this time. So in 1940, he disbanded his big orchestra to concentrate on free lance arranging, in spite of the fact that at the time many a lover of

the big band movement vehemently maintained that Redman, as a leader, had given the era as much impetus as had Fletcher Henderson!

Once he had given up as a leader, "the Little Giant," as he was known, fronted such groups only occasionally thereafter, most notably in 1946 and '47, for a European tour.

Ultimately—after 1951 to be exact, Redman worked largely as arranger and conductor for the singer/entertainer Pearl Bailey,* a close friend of Mrs. Redman. In 1954 and '55, Don also appeared in a small acting role in the Broadway show HOUSE OF FLOWERS, in which Miss Bailey starred.

"He was a brilliant musician and a marvelous writer," one jazzman said of Redman, "a man who always seemed a little uncomfortable fronting an orchestra, as if he felt he really belonged in the reed section—or behind an arranger's desk somewhere."

Don Redman was an important, a moving force behind the big band age, a master at fusing jazz and dance music while at the same time remaining so unobtrusive as to be almost unnoticed by the very ones who should have cheered him most.

*And also numerous singers on NBC.

Diminutive *Don Redman,* who stood tall among his musical contemporaries, is shown here with his big band. (Photo by courtesy of Mrs. Don Redman) PERSONNEL: (L to R) Sidney De Paris, Benny Morton, Shirley Clay, Fred Robinson, Manzie Johnson, Langston Curl, Claude Jones, Horace Henderson, Redman, Ed Inge, Talcott Reeves, Bob Carroll, Bob Ysaguirre.

The many-talented Don Redman, (July 29, 1900-November 30, 1963) who, out of friendship for Hoagy Carmichael, penned the verse for the song "Star Dust," (the portion beginning "And now the purple dust of twilight time. . . .") but who was never credited with his contribution to the song. *(Photo courtesy of Mrs. Redman)*

95

Don Redman and his orchestra, somewhere in Europe, 1946. (Photo courtesy Bertrand Demeusy) Personnel: Front row l to r: Buford Oliver, drums; Ray Evans, Pete Clark, Chauncey Haughton, Don Byas, saxes. "Peanuts" Holland, trumpeter, is hidden by Haughton. Trombonist at far right is Tyree Glenn. Other members unidentified.

CHAPTER XIX
The Jeter-Pillars Band

Whether white or colored, orchestras with more than one leader are extremely rare. The Dorsey Brothers, the Hudson-DeLange Orchestra, the Coon-Sanders Nighthawks, the McFarlane Twins—all of them white bands—are examples which come to mind, but all of those lasted only a few years.

It is surprising then, that of all such groups, the one which lasted longest is among the least known—a Negro outfit called the Jeter-Pillars Band.

Collectors of photos of America's great musical groups search eagerly for pictures of the Jeter-Pillars aggregation. It's strange that such keepsakes are rare; the band lasted more than a decade, and was photographed frequently. Such a paucity of pictorial material is all the more surprising in the light of the fact that both its former leaders are alive today.

James Jeter, one-half of the famous pair, spoke of the band recently amid a flood of pleasant memories. Now 63, he attended public schools in his home town of Little Rock, Arkansas and, later, Philander-Smith College, in the same city. He studied music privately, eventually mastering alto and baritone saxes to a degree which inspired him to apply for a job with the Alphonso Trent band, then an important Midwestern group out of nearby Fort Smith. Soon after Trent had hired the young saxophonist, the band moved into a long run at the Adolphus Hotel, Dallas, where they were joined by Hayes Pillars, a boyhood friend of Jeter's.

Jeter himself describes what happened after that.

"During the Depression—back in '31, or around there," he begins, "the bottom fell right out for Trent's band. The Depression got it, like it got a lot of other businesses.

"We were headquartering out of Pittsfield,

Massachusetts, in the thirties. It was real tough going, and we just couldn't make it. The band split up.

"Pillars, his brother Charles, and I were the entire reed section of that band (Trent used just three reeds). Well, we went to Cleveland, where a friend of ours got us a little job at a night club—seven of us—and that's how our own band got started."

Good fortune favored the Jeter-Pillars combo from the very start. Soon afterward, the group was offered a six weeks' booking at the Club Plantation in St. Louis—a run which eventually turned into a ten years' stay!

"The original group we had," Jeter recalls, "included the trumpet man Harry 'Sweets' Edison, and the great bass player Walter Page. We also had Jo Jones on drums, who came to us from Basie's band, but went back with Basie once the Count started moving up. That was along in 1934—or maybe 1935.*

"That Club Plantation thing," Jeter continues, "was our first important job, you see. But in the summer, when the place closed down, we'd travel a little bit, and that helped the band become even better known. From 1934 to 1944, though, that place was our home base, you might say. As they enlarged the club, we enlarged the band. We came in with seven men, and grew to a 12- or 14- piece outfit by about 1936 or '7. That was about the time—1936—when we all went to Chicago to cut a record, for Brunswick, of the band's theme song, 'Lazy Rhythm'."

"Gee, we had some fine men in that band," Jeter says. "Remember Big Sid Catlett, the drummer? He was with us. And so was Peanuts Holland, 'though he didn't stay long. He came with

*This apparently must have been in late 1935, since the Basie band was not formed until then.

us from Trent's band, you know."

Leonard Feather and other jazz writers have tended to discredit the Jeter-Pillars unit as a jazz organization; however it was capable of producing quite creditable examples of that type of music, when the occasion warranted.

"We were really rather versatile," Jeter says. "We could go down on the other side of the track, as the saying goes, and get right in the groove with those people, and then turn right around and go into a nice room or cafe, and play music there, too. We also did well behind floor shows, for which we were quite noted, including a lot of shows which Ziggy Johnson produced."

With a big book of varied arrangements, some by the noted Sy Oliver, who was a long-time friend of both Jeter and Pillars, and with still others by the Jeter-Pillars pianist John Carter, the orchestra found a wide audience, making frequent appearances at the big "Y Circus" in St. Louis. Such bookings permitted the group to remain a top-flight "territory" band, active until well past World War II.

"In 1945 and '6," Jeter indicates, "we got a job with the USO, playing shows for our GIs in the South Pacific. We did a lot of 'island hopping' on the so-called 'khaki circuit', and it helped our band's morale as much as that of the audience, believe me!"

The Jeter-Pillars orchestra returned to a changed America, however. By 1946, night club profits had fallen sharply, the "Live-it-up—Forget-the-war" spenders gone, and the big band age stumbling to an end.

"Economics was the only reason why we disbanded the orchestra, back in 1947," Jeter explains. "Prices went up. Everything cost so much that the night club people couldn't make it and, as a result, couldn't pay the price necessary for a good-sized band. That's when combos took over."

It was a closing chapter, of course, which could have been written to explain the demise of many other fine bands of the period—economics and shifting public tastes combining to destroy a musical aggregation.

But though the band swings no more, the ending of the Jeter-Pillars partnership is nowhere in sight. In 1948, the two men found employment at the busy Anheuser-Busch brewing plant in St. Louis, where they still work, side by side, as always. There, over their lunches, they are still prone to talk about the "old days" when, with a little luck and a lot of determination, they brought a big band successfully through a great depression and a major war. Certainly such a feat is worthy of frequent recounting.

James Jeter and Hayes Pillars: Their Jeter-Pillars Band, which evolved in part out of the earlier Alphonso Trent Orchestra, was primarily a "territory band"; however, it achieved considerable fame when it toured the South Pacific during World War II, under the auspices of the USO. (Photo by courtesy of Duncan Schiedt)

After appearing in the Hollywood film *The Benny Goodman Story,* in 1955, *Lionel Hampton* toured overseas with his band, playing successful concerts in Israel, Great Britain, North Africa and Australia.

CHAPTER XX
Lionel Hampton

In the summer of 1936, Benny Goodman was told of a sensational 23 year-old drummer and vibes man named Lionel Hampton, who at the time was working at a Los Angeles cafe. Goodman went over to the cafe, listened and, liking what he heard, hired Hampton.

Because Goodman was at the peak of his popularity then, it almost appeared that he had discovered a brand new talent that day. That, of course, was not the case.

Hampton, who had been born in Louisville, Kentucky, was reared in Chicago, where he played drums in the Chicago Defender boys' band. And, besides this early experience, Hampton came into the Goodman orchestra with an impressive background of employment with Paul Howard's orchestra, Eddie Barefield, and Les Hite. And some six years before Goodman ever saw him, Hampton (who was self-taught on vibes) had recorded a vibraphone solo of the tune "Memories of You," along with Louis Armstrong, in 1930. Four years afterward, he had gone out on his own—two full years before his Goodman tenure.

Even during his four years with the white clarinetist, Hampton frequently made recordings with "pickup groups" of his own choosing, featuring important sidemen from nearly every top-name jazz band in the country.

In September, 1940, financed partly by Goodman, he set out with a big band of his own, and created a sensation when he and his new orchestra played a break-in date at the world-famous Apollo Theatre in uptown Harlem. A young band full of promising soloists such as trumpeter Joe Newman, tenor saxophonists Illinois Jacquet and Dexter Gordon, and with Jack McVea on baritone, the orchestra possessed a rich, brassy sound, and featured sparkling solo work throughout.

On Christmas Eve of 1941, Hampton and his big band trekked over to the Decca recording studios and cut their first disc, "Just for You" and "My Wish." The following May, with essentially the same group, Hampton made a disc of "Flying Home," which he had cut twice before-once with the Goodman sextet, once with a 10-piece "pickup band".

That third recording of the tune established Hampton, for all time, as a dominant force in the world of the big band.

If there is any valid criticism of Lionel Hampton, it is perhaps a small one—namely, that by the late 1940s, he came to rely more and more upon excitement, upon noisy displays of kicking at the drums (in a fashion more befitting a boilermaker than the fine musician he was) in order to appeal to the audience. But in the light of the increasing popularity, by then, of rock 'n roll, his actions in this respect seem, in part at least, excusable because of economic necessity.

A man possessed of a wonderful beat, amazing energy, and the ability to produce beautifully disciplined big band performances, Lionel Hampton was, more than incidentally, one of the first jazz musicians to feature vibes. In addition to these accomplishments, he also introduced a delightful piano style all his own—that of using his two forefingers as he does his vibraphone mallets—by means of which he plays ferociously rapid passages in almost machine-gun fashion.

It is perhaps surprising then, that after more than a quarter century as a bandleader (and a great one, at that) so few people think to name the big orchestra led by talented Lionel Hampton as one of the very top Negro groups of our time.

A trio representing several million dollars' worth of talent: Louis, Ella, Lionel!

Composer Otto Cesana conducts the *Lionel Hampton Orchestra* in Cesana's composition "Symphony in Jazz". This Photo dates from about 1949. (Photo courtesy of *International Musican*)

CHAPTER XXI
Cab Calloway

"Oh, hi de hi-i-i de hi!"

When Cabell "Cab" Calloway, the 24 year-old singer from Rochester, New York, stood before a primitive Brunswick recording microphone in March, 1931, and "scat sang" his way through "Minnie the Moocher," he probably little suspected that with that one recording, his days as a relatively unknown entertainer were behind him. But once he discovered that fact, he and his vocalizing went completely beyond the bounds of even mild restraint.

Calloway and his sister Blanche had parted professional company several years earlier, she to form, successively, a group of orchestras which she called "Blanche Calloway and her Joy Boys,"* he to become part of a song-and-dance act in Chicago, where both he and Blanche had grown up.

While still in Chicago, a band called "Marion Hardy and his Alabamians" came into the Windy City, and in 1928, Calloway took over as leader, moving the band into New York City in 1929, just a year after he had assumed the leadership of the group.

But Calloway's tenure as leader of the Alabamians was a brief one; in that same year he assumed the leadership of another existing orchestra, this one called the Missourians, a 12-piece band which included R.Q. Dickerson, Lamar Wright and Reuben Reeves on trumpets; DePriest Wheeler and Harry White on trombones; William Blue, Andrew Brown and Walter "Foots" Thomas on saxes. The pianist was Earres Prince; banjoist, Charlie Stamps; tuba player, Jimmy Smith and the drummer LeRoy Maxey.

On June 3, 1929, the Missourians cut their first four recordings, "Market Street Stomp," "Ozark

*In March, 1931, Miss Calloway's group, which recorded several sides for Victor in Camden, N.J., was in reality Andy Kirk and His Clouds of Joy, a band which Blanche "picked up" at the Pearl Theatre, Philadelphia. She wanted to keep the band as her own; however, Andy and most of his men went their own way, only a couple of them remaining with Blanche.

Mountain Blues," "You'll Cry for Me" and "Missouri Moan," all of them for Victor in New York City. Even at this time Calloway ostensibly was the leader of the band; however, the discs from that session and two subsequent ones, as well, were released simply as "The Missourians," with Calloway's name not being appended to the record labels until a Brunswick recording date late in July, 1930. After that, the band maintained a busy schedule in the studios, nearly 50 sides in less than three years, the total output being released in America and abroad on some seven different labels.

Included among the varied output of Cab Calloway and his Missourians between 1930 and '32 were some of their most popular and best-remembered recordings, which vied with Cab's unique "Minnie the Moocher" as top sellers: "Mood Indigo," "I Got Rhythm," "St. James Infirmary," "Basin Street Blues," "Star Dust," "Kickin' the Gong Around," "Corinne Corinna," and, finally, an obvious followup to Cab's earliest hit—a tune titled "Minnie the Moocher's Wedding Day".

Musicians, who never have taken lightly to non-musicians joining their tight little society, were quick to point out that Calloway neither could read music nor play any instrument—that he was, in short, merely a very animated singer, and, many said, not such a good one, at that. But the dancers who paid their admissions, and the phonograph owners who bought the discs, could hardly have agreed less with Calloway's detractors, who often spoke derogatorily, too, of the hi de ho man's temper, too.

In 1941, Calloway's anger flared abruptly when, during a stage show, he accused one of his trumpeters, Dizzy Gillespie, of hitting him with a spitball. As a result of the fight which ensued, Calloway somehow received a cut across the seat of his pants—injuring something more than his trousers.

The early 1940s were the times of restless ferment of progressive jazz; even then, Calloway would have no traffic with the experimental form. At rehearsal, when Gillespie would occasionally present a short example of the new jazz, Calloway would be heard to stop the band and shout, "I'm not paying you to play that damned Chinese music!"

As World War II exploded all around our troubled planet, the Calloway records continued to be stacked in great piles onto record counters everywhere, and to be just as quickly purchased by "the final jury". "Hold Tight" and "Jumpin' Jive" (both of them featuring Cab's vocal antics) kept cash registers popping, as the Missourians filled a fatiguing round of personal appearances at the Zanzibar, at Frank Daley's Meadowbrook, and other noted dance centers, a routine they alternated with occasional visits to Hollywood for appearances in such films as "Big Broadcast of 1933," "Stormy Weather" and "Sensations of 1945".

Calloway continued to lead a successful big band until well into 1948, its personnel during its 20-year history including Illinois Jacquet, Chu Berry, Jonah Jones, Cozy Cole and Eddie Barefield—the latter of whom was, for the most part, the actual director of the Calloway band.

Behind the orchestra lay nearly 20 years of impressive public favor—a remarkable record for any song-and-dance man to have rolled up in the history of American music.

Since 1950, Cab Calloway has led numerous orchestras, large and small, the most recent a big band which enjoyed a successful run at the Mark Twain Riverboat, New York City, in the spring of 1966. And also, in the period of 1952 to '54, Calloway further distinguished himself by assuming the role of Sportin' Life, in the stage presentation of Gershwin's *Porgy and Bess*, which toured both the U. S. and abroad.

Whatever the critics may think of the vocal abilities of Blanche Calloway's brother seems unimportant here, for Cab Calloway managed to operate a profitable big band until well into a period when many others had long since quit. And in doing so, he gave some superb musicians an attractive showcase in which to display their talents, too.

Although not a member of Cab Calloway's big band, *Lena Horne* was accompanied by the "Hi de ho" man and his orchestra in the film "Stormy Weather." The amused-looking tenor saxophonist at left is Illinois Jacquet. (Photo courtesy 20th Century-Fox)

Almost every American knows the name of Cab Calloway. A smaller number recall Cab's sister Blanche and her various orchestras, but very few know about the "Hi De Ho" man's younger brother *ELMER CALLOWAY* who led this big band, prominent in the Washington, D.C. area in the 1920s. Elmer's trombonist Fred Norman, later to achieve considerable fame with Claude Hopkins, was one of the principal arrangers for young Calloway's group! (Photo courtesy of Fred D. Norman) PERSONNEL: PIANIST UNIDENTIFIED. SAXES: WIL-

LIAM SMITH, RAY FORREST, JOHN HARRIS. BASS, JOHN STEWART LEADER, ELMER CALLOWAY. DRUMS, PERCY JOHNSON. TRUMPETS: JOE HENRY, BOBBY WOODLIN, VAL VALENTINE. ACCORDION, HENRY BOWEN. TROMBONE, FRED NORMAN. (PHOTO AND IDENTIFICATION OF PERSONNEL, FRED D. NORMAN)

Best remembered of *Cab Calloway's* bands in his 1941 assemblage — comprising some outstanding jazz stars! (Photo courtesy Hilton Jefferson) PERSONNEL: (FRONT ROW) CALLOWAY, LEADER/VOCALIST; JERRY BLAKE, CLARINET/BARITONE SAX; HILTON JEFFERSON, ALTO; ANDY BROWN, ALTO; WALTER "FOOTS" THOMAS, TENOR. (SECOND ROW): DANNY BARKER, GUITAR; KEG JOHNSON, TYREE GLENN, QUENTIN "BUTTER" JACKSON, TROMBONES; (BACK ROW): DIZZY GILLESPIE, LAMAR WRIGHT, JONAH JONES, TRUMPETS.

In 1939, the talented singer *JUNE RICHMOND* was part of Cab Calloway's band, when it was playing at the Cotton Club in New York. Still later, she joined the Jimmy Dorsey outfit and, after that, Andy Kirk's orchestra. (Photo courtesy of Harold Blanchard)

One of the latter-day versions of the Cab Calloway Orchestra, with the outstanding drummer Cozy Cole featured. (photo courtesy of Hilton Jefferson) PERSONNEL: (Back Row): Palmer Bros., Vocal Trio; Cozy Cole, Drummer; Lammar Wright, Trumpet; Unidentified Trumpeter; Shad Collins, Trumpet; Jonah Jones, Trumpet. (Second Row): Danny Barker, Guitar; Keg Johnson, Trombone; Unidentified Trombonist; Quentin "Butter" Jackson, Trombonist. (Front Row) Benny Payne, Piano; Cab Calloway, Leader/Vocalist; Milton Hinton, Bass; Teddy McRae, Sax, Unidentified Sax Player; Hilton Jefferson, Sax; Andrew Brown, Sax; Walter "Foots" Thomas, Sax.

CAB CALLOWAY AND HIS MISSOURIANS, probably about 1931. (Photo courtesy Harry Dial) PERSONNEL: (Left to Right) Benny Payne, Reuben Reeves, R.Q. Dickerson, Jimmy Smith, Lamar Wright, Sr., De Priest Wheeler, Cab Calloway, Arville Harris, Leroy Maxey, Andrew Brown, Walter "Foots" Thomas. (Member at far right unidentified) possibly is Morris White)

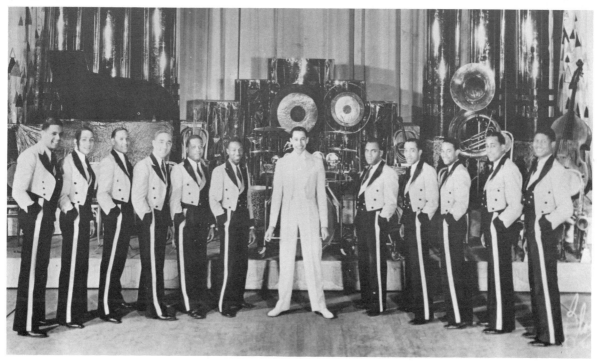

Although he declared himself bankrupt in 1941, *Claude Hopkins'* orchestra, only a few years earlier, **had been one of the** most popular in America. This early-day photo of the orchestra on stage at Roseland Ballroom, dates from the period of the greatest popularity of the band. (Photo by courtesy of Hilton Jefferson)

The trombone section of the *CLAUDE HOPKINS ORCHESTRA,* 1937: Fred Norman, Floyd Brady and Vic Dickenson. (Photo courtesy of Fred Norman)

CHAPTER XXII
Claude Hopkins

Already there have been several generations of jazzmen since the term "jazz"—or "jass," as it was earlier called—came into being not long after the turn of the century. But it was the musician born soon after the turn of this century who reached maturity at the time when jazz was in its golden age. Claude Hopkins, born in Washington D.C. on August 3, 1903, was one of these fortunate ones.

The child of parents who were both members of the faculty of Howard University, Hopkins might well have gone the route of the concert stage since he had early classical instruction as a pianist, and earned an AB degree at Howard. Instead, when he was 21, he joined Wilbur Sweatman's large semi-symphonic orchestra and in company with that group, travelled to New York, in 1924.

Late the following year, Hopkins had an opportunity to make a European tour as musical director for Josephine Baker, a position which kept him on foreign shores for nearly two years, following which he returned to Washington—the city of his birth—and where he immediately organized a small orchestra of his own, moving it into the Crystal Cavern in Washington, for an extended run.

In 1930, a band which had earlier been fronted by Charlie Skeets came under Hopkins' baton and, with it, a job at the Cocoanut Grove in Harlem. A short time afterward, a big break came when the band was booked into the great Savoy Ballroom.

Only a year after that, Hopkins landed a booking at Roseland Ballroom, where he continued to appear with considerable regularity for the ensuing four years. During that time, in 1932, particularly, the Hopkins group were great favorites at the Savoy Ballroom, as well.

Roseland Ballroom was (and still is) a favored dance spot of the nation, although regretfully it has been many years since a Negro orchestra played there. Such was not the case, however,

when Hopkins' band was enchanting Roseland customers with its big book of arrangements, among which were many by the immensely talented Fred Norman (a trombonist with Claude's aggregation from 1932 to 1938) and still others by Hopkins himself.

An almost immeasurable benefit accruing to orchestras which played the Savoy and Roseland ballrooms certainly was the network wire—a permanent telephone line over which radio broadcasts were carried directly from the dance halls to network headquarters in downtown New York, and from there to network affiliates all across the nation. In the final analysis, the publicity which orchestras derived from these late-night broadcasts was probably greater than any orchestra leader, Hopkins included, dared admit. For while Hopkins and his group seldom travelled beyond the environs of the city of New York, such broadcasts paved the way for the phonograph discs which followed—familiarizing the radio public with Hopkins' music in spite of the fact that many such listeners were never to know the Savoy or Roseland as anything other than magical names of never-never places from whence emanated magnificent music by way of tall, spindly-legged Crosley or Atwater Kent radios.

But in spite of frequent broadcasts, the piano artistry of Hopkins, and the talented sidemen—clarinetist Edmond Hall, trombonists Vic Dickenson and Fred Norman, trumpeter Jabbo Smith—the band was unable to survive for long.

The causes of the breakup are numerous, and a confused picture emerges as to the reasons.

"Prior to the demise of the orchestra," one former sideman declares, "we left Roseland for what was supposed to be a season at the old Cotton Club in Harlem. The band had changed personnel quite a bit by then, and maybe that was part of the trouble. Anyway," continues the musician, "at the end of the season, we went on tour with a 'Cotton Club Revue'—a big show which lasted just one week, even though it featured the Nicholas Brothers, Lena Horne and other top names."

Alone now with only his orchestra to sustain him, Hopkins quickly changed plans: Since the revue was finished, the leader chose to stay on the road.

The decision proved an unfortunate one. The tour which followed developed into a rugged, wearying series of one-nighters, from which the orchestra returned discouraged and debt-ridden.

Soon after the tour, like the Cotton Club Revue with which it had started out, the orchestra disbanded.

During World War II, Hopkins worked in an aircraft plant and, after the war, with Red Allen and a small combo at New York's Metropole Cafe. A seven-piece combo job in Catskill mountain resorts followed that.

Claude Hopkins still lives in New York and fortunately for music lovers is still actively leading small and excellent musical groups. Hopefully, there may come a day when he will choose to once again front a big band.

Clustered about *CLAUDE HOPKINS* (shown seated at keyboard) are the other members of the 1937 Hopkins band. (Photo courtesy of Fred Norman) PERSONNEL: (FRONT ROW, L TO R) JABBO SMITH, TRUMPET; VIC DICKENSON, TROMBONE; BEVERLY WHITE, VOCALIST; BEN SMITH, SAXOPHONE; JOE JONES, GUITAR. (STANDING, REAR ROW, L TO R): ABE BAKER, BASS; GENE JOHNSON, SAX; SHIRLEY CLAY, TRUMPET; BOBBY SANDS, SAX; CHAUNCY HAUGHTON, SAX; FRED NORMAN, TROMBONE; LINK MILLS, TRUMPET; PETE JACOBS, DRUMS.

CHAPTER XXIII
Jimmie Lunceford

By the time bandleader Jimmie Lunceford died, July 13, 1947, in Seaside, Oregon, the big band vogue was past.

Lunceford's death occurred under circumstances which were open to some question; it is said that there were whispered comments by some of the sidemen that Jimmie was poisoned. His death certificate, however, listed the cause as a heart condition, the term perhaps having a touch of tragic irony about it.

Born in Fulton, Missouri, June 6, 1902, Jimmie Lunceford grew up in Denver, Colorado, where he took lessons on trombone, clarinet, flute, guitar and saxophone.

In the Denver of the mid-1920s, there were but two large orchestras, one of them a white band led by a "Professor" Loman, the other a Negro orchestra headed by George Morrison. In the latter band, Jimmie Lunceford gained his early professional training, as did Andy Kirk, who was also in Morrison's band then.

Denver was not a good town for musicians, with the result that Morrison and Loman had to scramble for whatever musical jobs arose. Occasionally, however, when good luck favored, Morrison came up with two jobs on the same day. In such cases, he would assemble an extra band, and dispatch either Kirk or Lunceford to act as leader of the temporary aggregation.

But ultimately, Lunceford came to feel restricted in Denver, and moved on, working in the bands of Wilbur Sweatman and Elmer Snowden, in New York. Later, he attended college at Fisk University, where he majored in music, eventually earning a BA degree which enabled him to get a position as music instructor at Manassas High School, Memphis, Tennessee. There, while he labored at directing his youthful musicians, Jimmie discovered, in his classes, a group of highly talented young jazzmen, and these he fused together into a dance orchestra which soon began playing for local functions.

When his musicians completed high school, Jimmie encouraged them to enter college at Fisk University where, by good fortune, he then was able to obtain an instructor's position. Thus, when the Manassas graduates entered music classes at college, there was Lunceford, ready to continue instructing them, and to front the dance orchestra which, ultimately, paid the students' tuitions.

On June 6, 1930, Victor records cut the first Lunceford recordings, "In Dat Mawnin' " and "Sweet Rhythm". Made at Memphis, Tennessee, and labelled as "Jimmie Lunceford and his Chickasaw Syncopators," the discs—which have been reissued from time to time—reveal a developing two-beat sound by a 10-piece orchestra, the personnel of which included Willie Smith, Jimmie Lunceford and Earl Carruthers on saxes, Edwin Wilcox on piano, Jimmy Crawford on drums and Moses Allen on bass.

A widening territory, coupled with pleasantly encouraging sales of Lunceford's discs made possible two new moves by the young bandleader: He was able to enlarge the band slightly, and—when his student-sidemen completed college—resign his teaching post to make bandleading his full-time occupation.

In 1933, the Lunceford band acquired the services of a talented young arranger/trumpeter, Sy Oliver, who had earlier worked with the bands of Zach Whyte and Speed Webb. Not long after he joined Lunceford, Jimmie's orchestra began playing many Oliver arrangements, curiously swinging charts which were to continue pouring into the band's library for some six years afterward—"Dream of You," "Four or Five Times," Swanee River," "My Blue Heaven," "Organ Grinder's Swing," and "Ain't She Sweet?", to name but a few. There were humor, drive and sustained excitement inherent in Oliver's arrangements, and Jimmie's men translated them brilliantly.

And as was the case with most other big bands, Lunceford bought arrangements from many arrangers. Edwin Wilcox, Jimmie's long-time pianist, contributed heavily to the Lunceford book, his efforts including "Impromptu" and "Rhythm is our Business".

Lunceford had not only an enthusiastic, showmanlike band, but one which possessed an immense variety of music, ranging from the frenetic, fastpaced theme "White Heat" to classical melodies, tastefully tailored for dancing.

Even the Lunceford vocalists were chosen to give appeal to a wide range of tastes—Dan Grissom to carry the day when a sweet, commercial ballad was called for, Sy Oliver to handle the jazz vocals, and a trio of sidemen from the band to take care of novelty tunes such as "Margie".

Lunceford, quick to recognize the value of a flashy band, drilled his men so thoroughly that when his brass section reached a musical passage requiring the smart, flashing "do-wah" effects created by waving metal derby mutes before the bells of the horns, all of the mutes moved in precisely matched unison! Such devices gave the band considerable visual appeal, of course.

In the middle 1930s, the white trombonist Tommy Dorsey quarrelled with his brother Jimmy (a not uncommon practice with the pair), and as a result, withdrew from the band which he had been co-leading, setting off on his own. Another white bandleader, Joe Haynes, had the band Tommy wanted; Lunceford had the arranger. Eventually, Dorsey ended up with both.

Oliver's departure from Lunceford's band, in October, 1939, was virtually a mortal blow to Jimmie's organization, although the final effect of that loss was not to be felt immediately.

Indeed, two years after, Warner Brothers featured the Lunceford orchestra in a full-length feature, BLUES IN THE NIGHT, making it appear to many outsiders that the loss of Oliver might have no effect.

Unfortunately, however, the big band age was slowly ending, and what enthusiasm remained for large aggregations was undergoing a change of taste, the strutting, two-beat sound of the Jimmie Lunceford Orchestra receiving unexpected competition from dance bands which began adding gigantic string sections—whole rows of whining violins such as those in the bands of Harry James, Tommy Dorsey and Artie Shaw. The tempo of the music, and the era, was slowing. Swing was being diluted. Lunceford's day was past.

Still the orchestra struggled along, relying mainly upon the "old reliables" among both its men and its arrangements, although the task seemed hopeless. With the mid-1940s, the number of ballrooms in the nation shrank alarmingly, and bookings for big bands became fewer. Now, too, only an occasional recording date was available to the band, and even that would be for a minor record label.

In 1946, however, the fortunes of the Lunceford band slowly took a turn for the better. Bookings began to increase somewhat, and a comeback suddenly appeared imminent. It was a moment of encouragement cut short in the mid-summer of 1947, when the bandleader suddenly passed away, leaving trumpeter Joe Thomas and pianist Edwin Wilcox to hold together the band long enough to "play out" the bookings which remained on the calendar of advance dates.

The magic name of Jimmie Lunceford. The exciting sound of the big band with the two-beat rhythm, the precise, exciting sound. All these were gone and, perhaps saddest of all, it was a long time before most of the American public came to realize fully, just how much it had lost.

The Jimmie Lunceford Orchestra, as it appeared about 1935. Lunceford's was one of the most disciplined, best-appearing bands of its time. (Photo by courtesy of Francis Williams) PERSONNEL (STANDING, L TO R): RUSSELL BOWLES, TROMBONE; JOE THOMAS, TENOR SAX; EDWIN WILCOX, PIANO-ARRANGER; JAMES CRAWFORD, DRUMS; TOMMY "STEVE" STEVENSON, TRUMPET; SY OLIVER, TRUMPET-ARRANGER-VOCALS; EDDIE TOMPKINS, TRUMPET. (FRONT ROW, SEATED, L TO R): JIMMIE LUNCEFORD, LEADER; WILLIE SMITH, FIRST ALTO-VOCALS; AL NORRIS, GUITAR; MOSES ALLEN, BASS; HENRY WELLS, TROMBONE-VOCALS; EARL "JOCK" CARRUTHERS, BARITONE SAX. (PERSONNEL IDENTIFICATION BY COURTESY OF ANDY KIRK)

The talented, reserved and pleasant *Jimmie Lunceford,* (seldom heard as an instrumentalist with his band, save for the flute passage in the recording "Liza,") preferred simply to front his wonderful and swinging band. (Photo courtesy of Julian Hensley)

The man who poured some of the pure gold arrangements into the treasury of music of the Jimmie Lunceford band, trumpeter-singer-arranger *Sy Oliver,* as he appeared in the 1940's.

A dramatic shot of the great Jimmie Lunceford Band, during the time when the group was at the height of its popularity.

CHAPTER XXIV
Harlan Leonard And His Rockets

There seems to be a widespread opinion, at least among the lay public, that the greatest of the bands to be organized in the last half century reached the heights of success, rightfully trampling beneath them, the scores of lesser orchestras who, undeserving of fame, scrambled for the dance jobs which the name bands could not, or would not, fulfill.

It's a comforting belief, then one doesn't feel like pitying the underdog. There is one thing wrong with that, however: It isn't, in many cases, true that the deserving ones always make the grade.

Take for example the case of the delightful and talented Harlan Leonard Rockets, who left in their wake a massive trail of superb phonograph records as proof of their ability, some 16 selections of which, only recently, were assembled and reissued by RCA Victor as ready evidence that the Leonard band never achieved the fame it rightfully deserved.

Born in Kansas City in 1904, Harlan Leonard studied saxophone as a child, becoming so proficient that by November, 1924, he was a featured member of the Bennie Moten band during its earliest recording sessions, at one of which he appeared on the disc of "South".

Three years later Leonard, still with the Moten outfit, was among the personnel when they cut "Moten Stomp" for OKeh records, out in St. Louis.

Also in that orchestra was trombonist Thamon Hayes, who quickly became a close friend of Leonard's.

By 1931, Moten was rapidly altering personnel in his band, so Leonard and Hayes decided it was time to try their own hands at organizing a band. The joint venture, formed that year, took the name, "The Thamon Hayes Orchestra," and sped optimistically eastward to Chicago for a short run.

The orchestra failed to meet with much success, but managed to remain together, although sometimes precariously, until 1934, finally dissolving somewhat inauspiciously, with Leonard finally pulling together some of the former members into a band under his own leadership. That group lasted until 1937.

Not long afterward, back in Kansas City once more, Leonard had the opportunity to assume the leadership of still another big band, this one formed by Tommy Douglas.

Charlie ("the Bird") Parker was a member of that 1937 Harlan Leonard Orchestra, although "Bird" himself didn't remain even long enough to record with the Rockets. Drummer Jesse Price was with that band, too, as was Tadd Dameron, who joined in 1940. That was, of course, prior to the time of Dameron's unhappy commitment to the Federal hospital for narcotics addicts, in Lexington, Kentucky—days when Tadd's genius for arranging music was moving toward its inspired zenith.

And as if Dameron's arranging talents weren't enough for one orchestra, Leonard also wisely employed the services of James Ross, Richard J. Smith, Eddie Durham, "Buster" Smith and Rozell Claxton, all of whom helped to chart the band's way, musically.

In January, 1940, Harlan Leonard and his Rockets, 13 in number, journeyed to Chicago for their first recording session where, on the 11th of that month, they cut six sides for the Bluebird label, a subsidiary of Victor: "Rockin' with the Rockets," "Hairy Joe Jump," "Contact," "My Gal Sal," and "Skee".

This was roughly the same group which, in 1939 and '40, had played at the Savoy and the Aragon Ballrooms in Chicago, and just after their first record session, at the Golden Gate, the latter a night club in New York's Harlem area. The sax section of that band consisted of Harlan Leonard,

Darwin Jones, Hank Bridges, and Jimmy Keith. Trumpets in that group were Edward Johnson, William H. Smith, and James Ross. Trombonists were Richmond Henderson and Fred Beckett. Another William Smith—William S.—was the pianist; Effergee Ware was guitarist, Winston Williams the bassist, Jesse Price the drummer.

Three other recording sessions subsequently followed, with only minor changes in personnel, the last one in Chicago on November 13, 1940, at which time eight sides were cut, only four of which were ever issued.

It is perhaps more an indictment of the times than of the musical level attained by the Rockets which explains the demise of the organization, for it is a fact that few of the big orchestras which started cutting discs so late in the Swing Era ever survived long enough to achieve much lasting fame.

It is also a fact that the curtailment of travel, caused by Federal laws enacted during World War II, and the general shortage of top-flight musicians caused by the draft, hit the Harlan Leonard Rockets harder than many other such groups.

In 1944, with World War II still raging at its bitterest, Harlan Leonard finally decided to dissolve his fine orchestra, at that time not only an outstanding band, but an avant garde outfit which was already moving toward the middle of the long bridge between swing music and progressive jazz.

Leonard left music entirely, and moved away from the city of his birth, travelling all the way to Los Angeles and, ultimately, a job with the Internal Revenue Service, where he still works.

His trumpeter-arranger Richard Smith remains in Kansas City to this day, guiding the fortunes of the musicians local 627 there.

Along with Smith in K.C. are hundreds of other musicians—and music lovers—who know and remember "Harlan Leonard and his Rockets," and keep wishing that the Rockets' flight had lasted longer, much longer.

After his role as a sideman with Bennie Moten ended, *Harlan Leonard* assembled his own orchestra, "The Rockets," which achieved only minimal fame because they got off the ground rather late in the swing era. His was a fine band, nonetheless. (Photo by courtesy of Harlan Leonard)

Earl Hines, as he appeared early in his career as a bandleader. His piano stylings remain unique, yet unchanged basically, since the 1920's. (Photo courtesy of Francis Williams)

CHAPTER XXV
Earl "Fatha" Hines

There's a piano playing a tune called "Deep Forest". Then—

"Oh, Fatha! Oh, Fatha Hines!," a voice shouts.

"Ye-e-s?," comes a distant response.

Then the applause.

And with that, the brilliant pianist , Earl Hines comes jubilantly into the spotlight, his theme song introducing both his unique piano style and his big band.

At least that's how it was when Earl was among the foremost of the big jazz bands of the '20s, '30s, and '40s.

Jazz is the correct designation for Hines' music, for his band was more jazzlike than sweet-oriented—his keyboard stylings, incidentally, more trumpet-like than pianistic in nature.

His was a story punctuated in the far background by machine gun bullets, and lorded over by the suspicious eye of the Chicago mobs who ruled the night clubs and, for a long time, the contract which kept Hines working.

Though a child not of Chicago, but of Duquesne, Pennsylvania, Earl Hines made his reputation in the Windy City, during its most flambuoyant period—a time when a violin case wasn't always held in the arms of one who could play pianissimo without the need for a silencer.

It was a long way from the place where he was born, December 28, 1905; it was a while after his early studies on concert piano at Pittsburgh in 1914, to the huge "New Grand Terrace Ballroom" (said to be controlled by the Al Capone Gang) in the Chicago of 1928. Earl Hines, however, made the transition from Pennsylvania to the big city with ease and detachment, his connection with the gangsters extending no farther than his employment by them in one of their night clubs.

Back in Schenley High School, Pittsburgh, hardly a student who saw "Earl Hines and his trio" could have guessed that the leader of that little

triumvarate would ever scale the heights.

But by 1922, Earl Hines had escaped the smoky environs of the "Steel Capital," and was a full-time pianist with singer Lois B. Deppe, which took him for the first time in his life to Chicago.

There, in a five-year period, Hines worked with Carrol Dickerson, Sammy Stewart, clarinetist Jimmie Noone and, finally, Louis Armstrong.

By 1928, the big band was on center stage: Fletcher Henderson and some others had thrown big bands into high gear. A plethora of large ballrooms was springing up, dictating that a couple generations of Americans would thereafter settle for nothing less than a stageful of musicians.

So in December of that year, Earl Hines joined the movement with a big band all his own, and secured what he thought was to be a short-term engagement at the Grand Terrace but where, by edict of the Capone Dynasty, he was destined to remain for fully twenty years.

The recorded history of Earl Hines begins, though, with a series of old QRS records of piano solos, beginning in Long Island City, N.Y. on December 7, 1928, and continuing until February 13, 1929, when "Earl Hines and his Orchestra" began their recording activity over at the Victor recording studios in Chicago. At that time the Hines band comprised ten men, a group including Shirley Clay on cornet, William Franklin on trombone, Lester Boone and Toby Turner on altos, Cecil Irwin on tenor and Earl Hines on piano.

And though Wall Street was soon to witness a stock market decline of frightening proportions, the recording industry was still riding high when Victor engaged the Hines orchestra, for some fourteen sides—seven discs—were cut by the band that year—"Sweet Ella May," "Everybody Loves My Baby," "Good Little, Bad Little You," "Have You Ever Felt That Way?," "Beau Koo, Jack," "Sister Kate," "She's Funny That

Way," "Mississippi, Here I Am," "Chicago Rhythm," "It's a Precious Little Thing Called Love," "I'm Looking for That Certain Man to Love," "Glad Ŕag Doll," "Grand Piano Blues," and "Blue Nights".

But then came that black day in October, 1929, and the Wall Street tumble. With that, there followed nearly three years in which Earl Hines made no records whatever, but continued, however, to hold his big band together, and in enlarging the group, in 1932, to 12 men.

But besides the mere feat of keeping a large assemblage of musicians employed, Hines was keeping alive a very original piano style, as well, a style in which he used a sharp, single-note technique with his right hand, adding dynamics and tremolos to further augment his keyboard artistry.

Until the 1940s, Earl Hines was quite happy to drift along, resplendent in the title "Fatha Hines," which was given him one night when an exuberant young network announcer exclaimed, "Here comes 'Fatha' Hines, leading his chillun through the 'Deep Forest.'" The nickname "Fatha" has stuck ever since!

But by the 1940s, something was happening in American jazz, a movement which, at first, was called "Rebop," then "Bebop," and finally "Bop".

For a time, those who failed to harken to the cry of the "new sound" were trampled underfoot. Coupled with this development, Hines' band had for some two years or so been on a downhill slide.

Convinced that the modern jazz was destined to survive in spite of its critics (who were both numerous and vitriolic in their comments) Earl Hines was highly receptive to progressive jazz, and to its artists and those who sought to write arrangements in the new idiom, with the result that by 1943, he had attracted Charlie "Bird" Parker into his orchestra and, although Parker stayed only

until 1944, the alto saxophonist helped to steer the Hines band well on its way into the land of Bop.

With considerable speed, the earlier "Fatha" Hines book of arrangements became buried, first, beneath the newer orchestrations, then finally crowded out by such arrangements, written by Jimmy Mundy and Budd Johnson, both of whom were tenor saxophonists in the Hines reed lineup.

When singer Billy Eckstine, who had been with Hines since 1939, left to form his own Bop orchestra in 1944, he was joined by Sarah Vaughan, who had been second pianist to Hines, and his band's female vocalist. Charlie Parker also followed.

By late 1947, the promise which Bebop had seemed to hold was seemingly not to be fulfilled and, to make matters more serious, there was little chance to return to more prosaic arrangements; by then the big band was on its way out. So in 1948, Fatha Hines dissolved the large orchestra he had been leading for two full decades, and joined a small combo led by Louis Armstrong, another refugee from the large band format. Since that moment, Hines' career has been dominated solely by small-group jazz, culminating in the summer of 1966 with a tour of Russia by Hines and a combo. There, the pianist met with great success and considerable acclaim.

Earl Hines is today what he has been since the 1920s, a unique pianist—one of the truly great ones in the field of jazz. And though his swing-era arrangements were often too crowded sounding, too "busy" to swing as cleanly as they might have, and though his vocalists sometimes were not so musically adept as they might have been, the leader's superb piano magic always transformed the performance into music of the highest order.

It is no wonder, then, that Earl Hines deserves an important position in any listing of the memorable Negro dance bands.

A far cry from the type of music he played in the 1920s, (when he had composed the tune "Rosetta,") were the bebop sounds of *Earl Hines'* big band of 1943-4. In sharp contrast, too, were Hines' piano solos on records of this period, which were amazingly unlike the modern sound of his big band. Unfortunately, because of a musicians' union recording ban in 1943, what probably was Hines' greatest band never was recorded. This orchestra, gathered for Hines largely through efforts of his arranger/saxophonist Budd Johnson, included Dizzy Gillespie, Benny Harris, Gail Brockman, Shorty McConnell, Gus Chappell, Benny Green, Charlie Parker, Sarah Vaughan, Scoops Carey, Freddy Webster, John Williams, Julie Gardner, Andrew Crump, Jesse Simpkins and Benny Green. The drummer is Shadow Wilson.

THE EARL HINES ORCHESTRA, 1933, (Photo by courtesy of Duncan Schiedt) PERSONNEL: (TOP ROW) CHAS. ALLEN, TRUMPET; WALTER BISHOP, DRUMS; CECIL IRWIN, TENOR. (FRONT ROW) IDENTIFIED ON THE PHOTO ITSELF)

DIZZY GILLESPIE AND HIS "BOP" BAND, 1948. The man who wrote "Night in Tunisia," "Manteca" and "Salt Peanuts" was employing in this particular orchestra, such talents as those of trumpeter Benny Harris, bassist Al McKibbon, and saxophonists Ernie Henry and Yusef Lateef. (Photo by courtesy of Duncan Schiedt)

CHAPTER XXVI

Dizzy Gillespie

When Dizzy Gillespie and bandleader Cab Calloway had their famous altercation during a stage show, in September, 1941, and the fracas had ended in a little flashy knife play, Dizzy quite naturally was without a job!

So the bold young man from Cheraw, South Carolina, then 24 years old, joined Ella Fitzgerald, an association which lasted only a short time; by April, 1942, Dizzy was with Les Hite's orchestra. And a large part of the reason why the young trumpeter couldn't seem to keep a job could be explained in just one word: bebop!

For following a few childhood studies with his father, an amateur musician who died when little John Birks Gillespie was but ten, Dizzy had pursued rather prosaic musical studies at Laurinburg (N.C.) Institute and, late in 1934, at Philmore Hall, eventually adopting a swing style of trumpet playing which hewed rather solidly to a line earlier laid down by one Roy Eldridge.

But as Gillespie began slipping over to Minton's Playhouse, along in 1940, he started matching musical ideas with a group of other sidemen who, encouraged by Minton's manager, the ex-bandleader Teddy Hill, set up some exciting jam sessions during which, consciously or unconsciously, the participants began exploring new avenues in jazz. Chief among those experimenters, besides Gillespie, were Charlie "Bird" Parker, a drummer named Kenny Clarke, a pianist with the unlikely name of Thelonious Monk, and a great young guitarist named Charlie Christian. Out of those sessions grew the major ideas for the first new jazz form since swing. Moreover, those late night get-togethers gave Dizzy Gillespie a perfect practice ground on which to develop a technique of playing which, while technically astonishing, proved largely bewildering to the more conservative musicians who wandered into Minton's.

Convinced that the "new jazz" had something to say which should be heard in larger quarters, and spoken by a bigger voice, Gillespie allowed himself to be talked into joining Earl Hines' new band, in 1943, when Hines was experimenting with some of the new bop sounds. That tenure, like the Fitzgerald one, was brief, as were those with Coleman Hawkins and Mercer Ellington, which followed.

At last, a job opened up in January, 1944, at a club on 52nd Street in New York. Dizzy, together with tenor saxophonist Don Byas, pianist George Wallington, bassist Oscar Pettiford and drummer Max Roach, went to work in earnest. There, the new music, with its sudden rhythmic irregularity and calculated dissonance, created a sensation which stirred the ambitions of singer Billy Eckstine.

Eckstine approached Gillespie that summer, suggesting that Dizzy, functioning as "musical director," put together a large band under Eckstine's name—an opportunity which the trumpeter wasted no time in accepting. That orchestra, which nurtured bebop as had no other band before it, was a short-lived affair and, even before it folded in 1947, Gillespie was once again on his way back to New York—in the winter of 1944, to be exact—where the nucleus of the first 16-piece Dizzy Gillespie Orchestra was assembled by spring of 1945.

There were, besides Dizzy, four other trumpeters in the group: Kinny Dorham, Harry Pryor, Elmon Wright and Ed Lewis. Al King and Ted Kelly were the trombonists in that pioneering outfit, which utilized Max Roach as drummer, Lloyd Buchanan on bass, Howard Anderson on piano, and John Smith as guitarist. By then the accepted sax section was a five-man lineup. Dizzy was conventional in that respect, with Leo Williams and John Walker on altos; Charlie Rouse and

Lucky Warren on tenors, and Eddie De Verteuil, baritone.

There was something else conventional about Dizzy Gillespie's first big band venture: He tactly agreed to go out on a road tour of the South in company with a dancer, a comedian and a ballad singer!

Booked as "Hep-Sations of 1945," the new band met with a frigid reception among Southern audiences, who complained bitterly about the fact that the arrangements—mostly by Tadd Dameron and Gil Fuller—were just not dance music. The tour ended disastrously, with Gillespie salvaging a few of the remnants and heading for Hollywood with a combo, which played at a night club known as Billy Berg's. Audience reception there, too, was anything but cordial, so Gillespie returned to New York, where crowds were more receptive to the new jazz.

A record album, released by Victor on February 22, 1946 as "New 52nd Street Jazz,"* attracted a great deal of attention, outsold every other jazz album that year, and opened the doors for Dizzy Gillespie to assemble a second big band.

That orchestra, Dizzy says, " . . . was the first

*52nd Street, then called "Swing Street" was slowly dying as a center for music. This album was the final cry from what once was a major mecca for lovers of jazz.

jazz orchestra to hire a permanent conga player, and to play Afro-Cuban music." Moreover, it reunited Dizzy with many of his old friends from his Minton's Playhouse days—among them drummer Kenny Clarke and pianist Thelonious Monk. Added to that group of bebop originators were numerous other brilliant sidemen, including Chano Pozo on bongos, Cecil Payne on baritone, and Milt Jackson on vibes.

Gillespie's second big band foray lasted until 1950, followed by a six-year period in which the "high priest of bop" chanted his services against small combo backgrounds.

Then in 1956 a new and rather singular honor came Dizzy's way: He was chosen as the first band to represent this nation in a foreign tour sanctioned by the U. S. State Department. For that trip, Dizzy assembled his third and, to date, final big band, which remained together until 1959. A 16-piece group which included Quincy Jones, Benny Golsen and Jimmy Powell, it swept triumphantly through the Middle East, Asia and South America, playing arrangements by Ernie Wilkins, Quincy Jones and Melba Liston, and finding enthusiastic crowds wherever it went.

It was a remarkable climb for the high priest of bop; for by now the world proved to be full of his converts!

CHAPTER XXVII

And Other Voices*

The number of great Negro dance bands which have existed since the day when Fate Marable first walked up the gangplank of the S.S. New Orleans is truly astounding. Only a few, however, achieved national recognition, these being the hierarchy of a vast family of such organizations—some of the lesser known of which, surprisingly, spawned bands which went on to far greater success than the orchestras out of which they sprang.

From a handful of pioneering orchestras emerged numerous others. From George Morrison's band in Denver came Jimmie Lunceford, Andy Kirk, and a host of important sidemen, as well. From the Sykes Brothers band in Los Angeles came many more. Fate Marable, that Kentucky-born trailblazer of big bands, gave early professional experience to Louis Armstrong, Baby Dodds, Johnny St. Cyr and many others. From the Alphonso Trent band in the Middlewest came James Jeter and Hayes Pillars, destined one day to lead, jointly, an orchestra of amazing virility and lifespan—not to mention such other Trent alumni as Snub Mosley and Peanuts Holland. From the T. Holder orchestra came all of the original "Clouds of Joy" which Andy Kirk was to lead to fame. From Speed Webb's band there sprang, ultimately, the aggregations of Roy Eldridge and Chic Carter.

Such "parent" bands as these were veritable "hatcheries" in which dozens of other orchestras incubated, only to struggle into life as the whims of a fickle public—and a fluctuating economy—might dictate.

And through periods of prosperity, the need for big bands—for numerous such groups—was at its greatest. Unfortunately, a great number of such organizations just never achieved notoriety beyond their immediate territories. Who, for example, remembers Sammy Stewart's "Met" Orchestra, or the bands of Jimmy Bell, Clarence Jones, or Dave Peyton—all of whom were actively working, in the mid-1920s, in such Chicago entertainment centers as the Vendome, and at Ascher's Metropolitan Theatre, not to mention the Main, the Annex, and similar spots?

In this chapter, then, are just a few more of the many outstanding Negro dance bands, their existence recounted by photos and, in some cases, brief commentaries on their histories:

* * * * * * * *

BILLY BUTLER (THE SAVOY BEARCATS) In their book JAZZ . . . A HISTORY OF THE NEW YORK SCENE, authors Samuel Charters and Leonard Kunstadt describe the Savoy Bearcats band as " . . . one of the hottest around Harlem," and indicate that Duncan Mayers organized this jazz group nonpariel in Charleston, South Carolina in January, 1926, under the name "Charleston Bearcats".

One of the original members of that outfit, however, gives a different version: Demas Dean, a trumpeter with the group, names Mayers simply as the contractor for the band, and indicates that the Bearcats—at first a "co-operative" operation* was organized in New York under the musical direction of Billy Butler. Further, Dean gives 1924, not '26, as the year in which the band was formed.

In the original outfit were a tenor saxophonist named Raymon Hernandez, the leader/saxophonist/violinist Billy Butler, trombonist James Reevey, trumpeters Gilbert Paris and Demas Dean, pianist Leroy Tibbs, saxophonist Englemar Crummel, drummer Billy Lynch, banjoist Jimmy Green, and tuba player Chink Johnson.

Once organized, the group took a "break in" date at the Nest Club which, along with the Lenox Club and Small's Paradise, was a popular nightery

*A band owned by all the men who played in it, with each receiving an equal share of the profits.

with the "Ofays" (white audiences) who began making Harlem a part of their night club itinerary in the mid-1920s.

When the Savoy Ballroom opened, its management chose the Bearcats as one of a number of top-flight bands which it featured as initial attractions.

Changes were made in the band prior to the Savoy run, however, with Billy Butler stepping out and violinist Leon Abbey coming in as leader. A great Harlem pianist/arranger, Joe Steele, joined, as did alto saxophonist/violinist Otto Mikeel, banjoist Freddie White, and tuba player "Bass" Edwards. Alto saxophonist/clarinetist Carmen Jejo came in also, and the band felt that it was now ready to tackle the Savoy.

The ex-leader Billy Butler, in the meantime—who left the orchestra when internal dissension arose—moved on to Chicago. Less than three weeks afterward, he received a telegram, asking him to come back on his own terms—all this before Leon Abbey took over the band. "By this time, though," Butler reports, "I was merrily conducting Joe ("King") Oliver's orchestra at the Plantation . . . so I declined." For that reason, the Bearcats moved into the Savoy without Butler as their leader.

The opening of the Savoy in 1926, was truly a gold-plated affair, and thousands of dancers jammed the second floor of the big new building on Lenox Avenue, between 140th and 141st Streets, to see and hear the new Savoy Bearcats and an old Harlem favorite, Fess Williams and his great band. It was a crowd, a moment, a touch of fame that the Bearcats would never forget.

The same year, while they were still at the Savoy, they were signed to a contract by Victor. Several excellent recordings followed, including "Hot Notes," "Bearcat Stomp," and "Senorita Mine". But the best of the Bearcats' output on discs were "Stampede" and "Nightmare," two jazz recordings of such high calibre that they still rank along with some of the best so-called "hot" music of the 1920s.

With the steady flow of superb arrangements from the pens of Bearcat pianist Joe Steele, and such outside arrangers as Don Redman and Fletcher Henderson, the orchestra romped along, playing spirited charts of "Baby Face," "Hymn to

the Sun," "Poor Little Rich Girl," "Blue Room," and "Snag It," amid personnel changes which saw Joe ("In the Mood") Garland, trumpeter Bobby Stark and other sidemen come into the Bearcat fold, if only for a short time.

In 1928, however, just after the Bearcats had made a successful tour of South America, leader Leon Abbey had an opportunity to go to Europe, then highly receptive to jazz and to Negro bands, as had been the case since World War I.

But for one reason or another, the sidemen in the band were unavailable to Abbey for the trip, which was certain to prove a lengthy one.

The result was the demise of the Savoy Bearcats which, in 1928, disbanded almost as its leader packed to leave for Europe.

The sound hadn't lasted long, but while it had, it was a memorable one for Harlem—and for South America, as well.

LEON ABBEY'S BAND: When the Savoy Bearcats completed their engagement at the newly-opened Savoy Ballroom, they became "Leon Abbey's Band" and, in company with their leader, set out for a tour of South America, where Abbey had secured a job in a musical revue in Buenos Aires, Argentina. From there, the orchestra moved to a theatre in Montivideo for a month, then on to Rio de Janiero, for a two-month run at a theatre there.

Minor changes in personnel had been made prior to departure from New York. However, Demas Dean, Willie Lynch and Henry "Bass" Edwards all remained with Abbey. Pianist Joe Steele, on the other hand, withdrew before the trip, and started a small band under his own name in New York.

The South American junket lasted about a year. In that time, Abbey's band crossed the paths of several other Negro groups from America, among them the orchestra of Sam Wooding. In the talk which occurred, it was generally agreed that theirs was a time of enthusiastic acceptance for the Negro musician on foreign shores, convincing Abbey that he should strike out for Europe. Many of his men, however, showed no inclination to go along, and would have to be replaced before such a trip could be undertaken.

Thus it was that a revamped version of Abbey's band arrived in Paris a short time afterward,

126

opening with a short run at the Embassy Restaurant, then a longer one at the exclusive Florida Night Club where, according to Abbey, "Only the finest of champagne and rarest of wines were served . . . . " and " . . . . where one saw only mink coats, ermine, chinchilla . . . . and diamond bracelets . . .,the cream of society". There followed a two-weeks' leave of absence from the club, during which the band played for the King and Queen of Spain.

A dazzling round of other European engagements ensued: Deauville, Monte Carlo, Nice, then India, and the Hotel Taj Mahal in Bombay.

It was twelve years before Abbey returned to America. When he did so, he discovered that the band he had been fronting was if anything a bit small for American taste, for the big band vogue was then underway.

Hastily organizing such a group, he moved into a job at the Ubangi Club in New York and, still later, the original Cotton Club, then situated in Harlem.

Abbey himself describes what happened after that: "There seemed to be more work in the 'cocktail field,' " he explains, "so I disbanded the big band and organized a quartet which opened for six months at the Dixie Hotel, on 42nd Street, New York."

Since that time, Abbey has remained in music, leading small combos which are surprisingly popular, particularly in Chicago, where Abbey now lives.

THE TEDDY HILL BAND: According to Harold Blanchard, a saxophonist with the Teddy Hill Orchestra of the 1930s, Hill's was an unusually good group, at times numbering among its personnel such men as Roy Eldridge, Chu Berry and Dizzy Gillespie. Working principally at New York's Savoy Ballroom, however, the orchestra never achieved the nationwide fame it so richly deserved. Occasionally, though, it made the circuit of jobs which included the Apollo Theatre in New York, the Pearl and Lombard theatres in Philadelphia, and the Howard in Washington, D.C.–" 'rounding the world," as musicians of the era often referred to that junket.

But while the Hill aggregation was essentially a

territory band, it reached the ears of a nationwide audience through radio broadcasts and through a number of phonograph recordings, including sessions on the Perfect record label, 1935, Vocalion records, 1936, and Bluebird, 1937.

Hill, who had earlier played in the Luis Russell band, operated his orchestra in all for a mere six years. Gradually, as his interests shifted to other enterprises—among them the management of Minton's Playhouse in Harlem—Hill came to depend less and less upon his orchestra as a livelihood, with a result that in 1940 the group disbanded entirely, the remnants being taken over by drummer Kenny Clarke.

THE ELI RICE BAND: Eli Rice's was a Minneapolis outfit which featured the bandleader (who was also a fine singer) as its drummer. In 1929-30, the best years of this orchestra, it also featured such sidemen as trumpeter Joe Thomas, saxophonist Eddie Barefield and trombonist Keg Johnson.

The basic instrumentation of the Rice orchestra was two alto saxophones, one tenor sax, two trumpets, one trombone, and bass, piano and drums—the standard grouping of instruments for the mid-1920s, but one which was becoming less and less common by 1930.

THE WILLIE BRYANT BAND: By 1936, the depression was making it rough going for most of the big bands. Even though the repeal of prohibition helped to change the illegal speakeasies of the 1920s into the respectable night clubs of the '30s, opening them to a larger public, the high rate of unemployment in the U.S. served to quell the success of many clubs, even though public interest in big bands was running high.

Harlem's Ubangi Club carried on during this period, however, and frequently featured large orchestras, among them the band of Willie Bryant, at that time comprising Jack Butler, Wallace Jones, Johnny Duzzell, Stanley Payne, Shorty Hardin, George Matthews, Manzie Johnson, "Bass" Hill, Roger Ramirez, Charlie Frazer, Joe Thomas, Bobby Lessey and, of course, Bryant himself.

"That was a terrific band," recalls trumpeter Thomas, "with a lot of extra drive coming from its

127

arrangements—things written for the band by Charlie Dixon and Benny Carter."

THE GEORGE MORRISON ORCHESTRA: A pioneering band of the Denver area, the George Morrison Orchestra grew out of a trio which the leader organized in 1913. By 1920, it had become a big band, soon after which Morrison took the group to New York where it cut its first discs at the Columbia Phonograph plant.

A nationwide tour followed, including a successful engagement at the Carlton Terrace Supper Club in New York City. And though his was a good group, musically, and might well have become famous, Morrison believed that he was a more important "name" in his home territory, and so returned to Denver with his men. In the nearly 50 years since, he has operated a popular local band which includes some men who have been on the Morrison roster for as long as 40 years!

Morrison comes by his talent naturally: His father was one of the "King Fiddlers" of Missouri where George was born in 1891. By the time he was seven, he was a guitarist in a family musical venture, "The Morrison Brothers String Band". He was studying to be a concert violinist by the time he was only 13. In 1911, he married a Denver girl. The Morrisons have a son and a daughter, both musically talented.

George Morrison's was one of the first—and for a long time one of the only—Negro big bands in the Mile High City. His orchestra, down through the years, has provided many young musicians with their first opportunities to be heard professionally, the alumni of his band including such stellar names as Andy Kirk, Jimmie Lunceford, and Hattie McDaniel. Occasionally the Morrison family still presents concerts.

THE SHUFFLE ABERNATHY ORCHESTRA: This Milwaukee band, which included trumpeter Joe Thomas (1930 to '33) also comprised such sidemen as Jabbo Smith, Budd Johnson and Cookie Mason, and a white drummer, Gordon Heidrich. A 12-piece band, the group included the typical instrumentation of the middle-'30s: four saxophones, four rhythm instruments, four brass.

ZACK WHYTE AND HIS CHOCOLATE BEAU BRUMMELS: "Zack Whyte and His Chocolate Beau Brummels" was the amusingly original name of a Cincinnati band, one of several outstanding orchestras to play at New York's Alhambra Ballroom when it opened for the first time, in mid-September, 1929.*

Whyte's instrumentation at the time was the rather standard mid-1920s one: Two alto saxes and one tenor, two trumpets, one trombone, tuba, piano and guitar.

The Chocolate Beau Brummels' recorded output ranged from medium tempi selections such as "When You're Smiling" to sweet ballads such as "Goodnight, Sweetheart," and a sprinkling of blues, as well.

Through the ranks of the Zack (sometimes spelled "Zach") Whyte organization passed some outstanding sidemen, including Sy Oliver, Quentin Jackson and Vic Dickenson.

WALTER BARNES AND HIS ROYAL CREOLIANS: Trombonist Ed Burke disclosed recently that he was the organizer, in 1929, of the original Walter Barnes orchestra. He adds, however, that a violinist, Detroit Shannon, "fronted" the group before Barnes did. Organized in Chicago, the band soon secured a booking at the Marigold Ballroom, in that city. At first, it played only in the "Annex," a smaller room attached to the main ballroom. Later, because the band proved popular in competition against the white bands which played there, the management moved the group into the main ballroom.

Soon afterward Shannon withdrew hurriedly, following a dispute about money, and the orchestra was left without even a nominal leader. Since it was a co-operative outfit a vote was taken, and Walter Barnes selected to be the "baton waver," being as Burke describes him, "a virtuoso and a personality".

When the management of the ballroom suggested that a little fancier name than just "Walter Barnes and his Orchestra" might be helpful, Burke suggested that they pattern the name after the popular "Guy Lombardo and his Royal Canadians" by calling themselves "Walter Barnes and his Royal Creolians".

*Luis Russell, the Missourians, Benny Carter, and Charlie Johnson were the four other "grand opening" bands.

128

The Barnes orchestra, utilizing mainly head arrangements* and stock orchestrations supplied by music publishers, found itself so popular that it began recording for Brunswick Records. By 1930, it was ensconced at Al Capone's nightclub, the Cotton Club, in Cicero, Illinois, where, in fact, it was playing when police swooped in and broke up the establishment.

Some time later, while the orchestra was out on the road, Barnes became ill, as a consequence of which the band became one of several groups which, at one time or another, Lucius "Lucky" Millinder fronted under his own name.

In 1940, however, Barnes was again leading the band when the circuit of bookings took them to Natchez, Mississippi, and a ballroom job where they were to replace Earl Hines, who had cancelled his booking there.

During the evening of April 24th, a fire broke out in the ballroom, fed by dry moss, with which the room was heavily decorated. In a matter of minutes, the entire place was consumed by flames. Nearly 200 customers, including several of the musicians, Barnes among them, perished in the fire.

SAM WOODING AND HIS CHOCOLATE KIDDIES: Only six years after the revolution in Russia, Sam Wooding, an American bandleader, bravely decided to risk taking his large "symphonic jazz" orchestra behind the newly-fallen Iron curtain. Fears as to how the fledgling Soviet regime might deal with visiting Americans plagued Wooding and his men to such an extent that, as the leader himself reported it, "The next thing I knew, our drummer disappeared—sailed for home out of sheer fright! But we got a replacement, and we went to Russia."

The trip proved to be a high spot of the Wooding band's history, later to be climaxed by enthusiastic' audiences in Moscow, too. That reception, to a degree, was matched by later crowds in Berlin, Copenhagen, Barcelona, Paris and other major cities of the world, with the result that Wooding and his bands (variously known as "The Sam Wooding Orchestra" and "Sam Wooding's Chocolate Kiddies") spent years abroad thereafter, often featuring such famous sidemen as Tommy Ladnier, "Doc" Cheatham, "Big" Sid Catlett, Gene Cedric, and Reunald Jones.

One of the first Negro bands to bring jazz, in any form, to foreign countries, Wooding today is better known among foreign audiences than American ones, although at one time he was one of New York's truly fine Harlem pianists, even before the days of Fats Waller. And prior to his extensive travels abroad, Wooding and his orchestra were featured at the Club Alabam, the same cellar bistro which gave the Fletcher Henderson band its start.

Although Wooding's big orchestra disbanded many years ago, he and singer Rae Harrison still are active performers in Europe, appearing as a duo, often in German night clubs, and occasionally on television there.

FESS WHATLEY: In any volume about dance bands, there must surely be an honored place for the "starmakers," those men who help to develop the talents of many musicians. And "starmaker" certainly is a fitting accolade for John T. "Fess"* Whatley.

Born John Tuggle Whatley, in Tuscaloosa, Alabama, he and his parents moved to nearby Birmingham when John was twelve. There he received his education, primarily at Tuggle Institute, studying in such diverse fields as music, printing, plumbing and electrical engineering. Eventually, he became the bandmaster at the school.

Transferring, in 1917, to a similar position at Industrial High, Whatley formed a travelling orchestra—a "society type" group—made up mostly of the most talented of his young high school musicians.

From that time until the early 1960s, Fess Whatley led some outstanding dance bands, through whose ranks passed many men who later helped form the Erskine Hawkins band—Sammy Lowe and Paul Bascomb, among them.

Bandleader Teddy Hill is another alumnus of the Whatley bands, as are Curly Parrish (brother of Avery Parrish, pianist in Erskine Hawkins' group), trumpeter Shelton Hemphill, and such former Mills

*Arrangements "worked out" by the musicians without benefit of written manuscripts, the rough arrangement itself being more or less memorized by the individual musicians so that, by recall, the band could play the selection repeatedly in much the same fashion.

*The nickname is a shortened version of "professor".

129

Blue Rhythm* bandsmen as Scad Hemphill and the McCord brothers, Castor and Theodore.

And besides the numerous other ex-Whatley students who became bandmasters, a truly staggering number went out to become members of such orchestras as those of Ben Watkins, Lionel Hampton, Edgar Hayes, Jelly Roll Morton, Benny Carter, Lucky Millinder, Louis Armstrong, Don Redman, Chick Webb, Sam Wooding, Joe Steele, Ray Charles and countless others.

Fess Whatley—the man who started so many young men on their ways to productive lives in music—is retired now. There's a new elementary school in Birmingham, named in his honor, a solid and fitting tribute to the Starmaker of Alabama.

FESS WILLIAMS AND HIS ROYAL FLUSH ORCHESTRA:

The Fess Williams band, organized in Winchester, Kentucky, in 1919, continued in operation, in varying size, until 1946.

Williams, who was born in Danville, Kentucky, in 1894, began studying violin when he was 12, but switched to clarinet and, later, saxophone, during the time he was in Tuskegee Institute, beginning in 1910.

Like the Fess Whatley band, the Williams group grew out of the latter's activities as a high school music teacher.

In 1923, the Fess Williams aggregation, then a five-piece combo, left Kentucky to travel the nation. The larger band which evolved out of that quintet began recording for Gennett Records, in 1926.

During the lifespan of the enlarged orchestra—which played both at the Savoy and Roseland ballrooms, in New York—a number of famous sidemen worked in the group, among them Rex Stewart, Kenneth Roane, Hank Duncan and Jimmy Harris.

Besides writing most of the arrangements which his band played, Williams composed "Make Me Know It,"** Musical Camp Meeting," and several other compositions, at least one of which, "Hot Town," gave the band one of its best selling phonograph recordings.

*A band which evolved out of one of Horace Henderson's bands.

**Recorded in New York City, May 24, 1926, by a 7-piece version of the later Fess Williams big band.

This is the combo which violinist *Leon Abbey* fronted during his high school years, and which gave him bandleading experience which eventually carried him into the big band field. (Photo by courtesy of Leon Abbey)

Leon Abbey's Band in South America, 1927. Even the leader cannot identify all the men shown. In the reed section, however, are Prince Robinson and Joe Garland. The drummer is the late Willie Lynch. Nat Brown, also deceased, is one of the trumpeters; the other is Demas Dean, who now lives in Los Angeles. Trombonist is Bill Horton. (Photo courtesy of Leon Abbey)

Many of the orchestras out of the Midwest (save for the Kansas City groups) failed to reach the fame they well may have deserved — possibly because New York City spawned so many orchestras of its own, right in the shadow of the major recording studios so necessary to the fame of any band. That may be why JAP ALLEN and his group, which were a Midwestern outfit, never became widely known. (Photo courtesy of Duncan Schiedt)

Little known even in their heyday, and scarcely remembered now, are *WALTER BARNES* and his Royal Creolians, a Chicago band which was one of the first Midwest orchestras to make regular, annual tours of the South. (Photo by courtesy of Joe Mason) PERSONNEL: (Front Row) Ed Burke, Leon Scott, George Thigpen, Walter Barnes (Standing, Center) Urbie Gage, Leon Washington, Lucius "Chops" Wilson, (Back Row) Wm. Bradley, Otis Bates, Bill Winston (drums); Paul Johnson, Bill Thompson. (PERSONNEL IDENTIFICATION BY ED BURKE)

A portrait of *Eubie Blake* who, while active but a short time as leader of a big band, wrote such song hits as "Memories of You," such great shows as SHUFFLE ALONG and—in doing so—provided a wealth of music for America. (Photo courtesy of Eubie Blake)

132

Tiny Bradshaw and his Orchestra. PERSONNEL: (PARTIAL) STANDING, TINY BRADSHAW, LEADER; TENOR SAXES COUNT HASTINGS (LEFT) AND JOE ALLSTON (RIGHT END OF REED SECTION). THE TROMBONIST AT EXTREME RIGHT IS JACK RAGGS

Time has erased the memories of the names of many of the men in this 1921 photo of *Eubie Blake's* SHUFFLE ALONG Band, even in the mind of its leader. A partial list of personnel, however, is provided in the accompanying caption. (Photo by courtesy of Eubie Blake) PERSONNEL: (PARTIAL) JOHN RICKS, BASS; CARROL JONES, TROMBONE; RUSSELL "POP" SMITH, TRUMPET; GEORGE REGUES, DRUMS; WILLIAM GRANSTILL, OBOE; HALL JOHNSON, VIOLA; EUBIE BLAKE, CONDUCTOR.

A great band of the 1930's, but one which was never well known outside of the Harlem area of New York: *WILLIE BRYANT'S ORCHESTRA.* Bryant, a native of New Orleans, led bands off and on from the mid-1930's to the late 1940's. His orchestra's theme song, "It's Over Because We're Through," became its best known recording. (Photo courtesy of Duncan Schiedt)

Although best recalled as "the Father of the Blues," (he wrote "St. Louis Blues," "Beale Street Blues," and others) *W.C. HANDY,* who was born November 16, 1873, in Florence, Alabama, led countless big bands, most notably his "Handy's Orchestra of Memphis" which, in 1917, recorded a large number of sides for Columbia Records. A 13-piece outfit, that orchestra ultimately helped launch Handy on careers as a song publisher/composer. By 1958, though totally blind, Handy continued to operate his publishing business. In March of that year, he passed away. (Photo by courtesy of Duncan Schiedt)

In 1933, *Benny Carter*, long a respected alto saxophonist (he had been a sideman with Horace Henderson, Duke Ellington, Charlie Johnson, Chick Webb, and McKinney's Cotton Pickers) launched his first big band, which proved to be an on-again-off again affair, with the result that he is better remembered today as a great instrumentalist who, in spite of his somewhat unpredictable nature, has been tremendously successful at scoring motion picture sound tracks—an exacting task, to say the least. (Photo by courtesy of INTERNATIONAL MUSICIAN)

Not many Americans today, even dance band enthusiasts, can recall the *CHIC CARTER ORCHESTRA*. Carter, a singer-dancer, worked in Speed Webb's orchestra for a time. When Webb began to secure enough work to support two bands, he selected Carter to "front" the second one for him. Ultimately, as Webb prepared to retire from music, he gave many orchestrations to Carter, who carried on as director of the group he had been leading, but changed the name to "Chic Carter and his Orchestra." Ohio, Michigan and Indiana made up the prime territory travelled by the Chic Carter unit. The photo dates probably from about 1937, when the band was at its peak. (Photo by courtesy of William Mills)

The scene is Small's Paradise, a cellar dance place at 2294 7th Avenue, New York City. It is 1946, and a part of the *Chris Columbus big band*—a contingent called "The Mad Men," are the featured orchestra. (Photo by courtesy of Ray Copeland) PERSONNEL: BERNIE MACKEY, GUITAR; ARTHUR GOODLETTE, BASS; SONNY PAYNE, DRUMS; RAY COPELAND, TRUMPET; DON COLE, TROMBONE; HAROLD MITCHELL, TRUMPET; FLETCHER ALLEN, BARITONE SAX; RUDY WILLIAMS, ALTO SAX; "BO" MC CAIN, TENOR SAX.

"Mr. B.,"—*Billy Eckstine*— now remembered primarily as a singer, but once leader of one of a small handful of big bands which, in the 1940's, sold a brand of "way out" jazz called bop. (Photo courtesy of RCA Victor)

MARION HARDY AND HIS ALABAMIANS, probably about 1929. This was the band which became the first Cab Calloway Orchestra. PERSONNEL: Eddie Mallory and Elisha Herbert, trumpets; Charlie "Fat Man" Turner, tuba; Henry Clark, trombone; Jimmy McHendricks, drums; Marion Hardy, Artie Starks and an unidentified third reed man; Leslie Corley, banjo; Ralph Anderson, piano. Standing, with baton, is another unidentified member. (Photo courtesy Andy Kirk)

An informal photo of Duke Ellington's son *Mercer,* during the time that the young trumpeter was fronting his own big band, during the decade 1939 to '49. Sidemen in Mercer's band included, collectively, Dizzy Gillespie, Ray Copeland, and Clark Terry. Like his father, Mercer is a talented composer-arranger, his compositions including "Things Ain't What They Used to Be" and "Moon Mist." (Photo by courtesy of Ray Copeland)

"My band's no Mickey Mouse outfit", said the mighty *Coleman Hawkins* when New York's Danceteria tried to induce him to play stock arrangements of "Woodpecker Song" and "Playmates". With that retort, Coleman and his big band took leave of the place forever. His shortlived big band, formed in 1940, was a 16 piece group which played, among other places, Harlem's Savoy Ballroom, (Photo courtesy of RCA Victor).

Saxophonist *Les Hite,* although born in Du Quoin, Illinois (the year was 1903) was in Los Angeles by the 1920s, where he assumed the leadership of Paul Howard's Quality Serenaders in about 1930. Soon afterward, Louis Armstrong became "front man" for the band, which operated under Armstrong's name 1930 to '32, during which time Lionel Hampton was also part of the band. After Armstrong moved on, Hite remained active until the 1940s.

In its short history, the *Teddy Hill* band established an excellent reputation for its solid versatility, and for the fact that it frequently included among its personnel, some top-drawer jazz artists of the period. (Photo by courtesy of Gus McClung) PERSONNEL: (Seated, front row) Sam Allen, piano; John Smith, guitar; Howard Johnson, alto sax; Harold Blanchard, alto sax; "Chu" Berry, tenor sax. (Standing) Unidentified vocalist and Teddy Hill, leader/saxophonist. (Seated, second row) Gus McClung, trumpet; Bernard Flood, trumpet; Louis Hunt, trumpet; Joe Britton, Trombone. (Third Row) Bill Beason, drummer; Dick Fulbright, bassist.

Around Philadelphia, in the early 1930s, one of the most popular orchestras was that of *DOC HYDER,* a group in which trumpeter Taft Jordan got his start. (Photo courtesy Duncan Schiedt)

Another of the many big bands to emanate from the Harlem area of New York, The *Alex Jackson Orchestra.* (Photo by courtesy of Eubie Blake) PERSONNEL: 1st man unidentified; 2nd man Izzie Myers; 3rd man Edgar Sampson, alto sax; 4th man unidentified; 5th man is leader Alex Jackson; 6th and 7th unidentified; 8th, Horace Holmes; 9th unidentified; 10th, Steve Wright, drummer.

Out of this six-piece aggregation grew the 11-piece DEWEY JACKSON PEACOCK ORCHESTRA, which recorded briefly for Vocalion Records, in 1926. Trumpeter Jackson, one of the proud clan of musicians out of St. Louis, was born in that city in 1900. Beginning his professional career with an Odd Fellows' band when he was 12, he graduated ultimately to working in the riverboat orchestras of Charlie Creath and Fate Marable. The drummer has been tentatively identified as Harry Dial. (Photo courtesy of Duncan Schiedt)

BUDDY JOHNSON: At about the close of World War II. This bandleader was born in Darlington, South Carolina. His 15 piece band played frequently at the Savoy Ballroom and during the same period, toured the South as a rhythm-and-blues attraction. Although Johnson (who was a fine arranger) came to New York in 1938, he did not assemble a big band until 1944. His girl vocalist is worth more than mere mention; she was Buddy's kid sister Ella, a modern blues singer who is still almost totally unknown to the white public, yet a great favorite with audiences of her own race. (Photo by courtesy of Julian Hensley)

143

The trumpeter/trombonist/singer *MILTON LARKINS* (seated, center, front row) with his orchestra, a Chicago group of the late 1930s which during its career included trumpeter Wild Bill Davis and tenor saxophonists Illinois Jacquet and Arnett Cobb (Photo courtesy of Bertrand Demeusy)

Those who know *Louis Jordan* often recall him only for his "Tympani Five." But in 1951, he was fronting a big band which, unfortunately, came a bit too late in the era to achieve much fame.

144

The GEORGE E. LEE NOVELTY SINGING ORCHESTRA apparently was a small contingent taken from Lee's larger 10-piece group, both of which featured pianist/vocalist Julia Lee. This photo, possibly taken in Kansas City about 1929, includes Sam Auderbach, trumpet; George E. Lee, tenor; Julia Lee, piano; Abe Price, drums. Second from right is Chester Clark. Both the small and large bands of George E. Lee recorded for Brunwick, in the late 1920s. While Kansas City was the headquarters of the orchestra, Lee and his men travelled widely, particularly in the Southwest, and once were great favorites in New York, as well. (Photo courtesy of Duncan Schiedt)

One of several bands controlled or managed by music publisher-song writer Irving Mills was the *MILLS BLUE RHYTHM BAND* of the early 1930s. Although not widely remembered today, this group — or variations of it — recorded prolifically for such recording companies as Melotone, Vocalion, Brunsick, Banner, Perfect, and Victor. (Photo courtesy of Duncan Schiedt) PERSONNEL: (PARTIAL) Gus Aikens, trumpet (Middle row, just to the right of the drummer); Harry White, trombone (far right, back row); Crawford Weatherton, saxophone (lower right).

145

Trumpeter *CHARLIE CREATH* led an orchestra which was called by bandleader Andy Kirk, ''. . . one of the incubators from which came the sidemen for a lot of great bands.'' The size of Creath's band varied, but it kept going from 1916 to 1940, recording, along the way, for Okeh Records. Creath, who died in 1951, never led a famous big band, and is best remembered for his smaller groups, such as this one which includes (left to right) Sammy Long and Willie Rollins on C Melody saxes; Charlie's sister Margie Creath on piano, Charles Lawson on trombone, Charlie himself on trumpet, and Zutty Singleton on drums. (Photo by courtesy of Duncan Schiedt)

This is the *Bennie Moten Orchestra*, as it appeared during 1932, the time when it was at its best. Leader Bennie Moten was a native of Kansas City, Missouri, where he was born in late 1894. From about 1922 until he died, in 1935, (while undergoing a tonsillectomy), he continued to lead his band. His first orchestra was a small group which recorded for OKeh, his later, larger band recording for Victor, beginning in 1926. A composer as well, Moten wrote "South." When he passed away, the leadership of the orchestra passed into the hands of his brother Buster, the band's accordionist; soon afterward, however, it disbanded, with most of the members migrating to the Count Basie Orchestra. PERSONNEL: SEATED AT PIANO, LEFT, WILLIAM (LATER "COUNT") BASIE. LEANING ON PIANO, JAMES RUSHING, VOCALIST. DRUMMER, WILLIE MC WASHINGTON. BANJOIST, BUSTER BERRY. SAXES: JACK WASHINGTON, HARLAN LEONARD, VERNON PAGE. TROMBONES: EDDIE DURHAM, THAMON HAYES. TUBA, WALTER PAGE. TRUMPETS: ORAN "HOT LIPS" PAGE, BOOKER WASHINGTON, ED LEWIS. STANDING AT RIGHT: BENNIE MOTEN, SECOND PIANIST. CROUCHING AT RIGHT, POINTING, BUSTER "BUS" MOTEN, ACCORDIONIST/DIRECTOR.

Another view of the *Bennie Moten Orchestra*, this one taken at Fairyland Park Ballroom, Kansas City, in about 1930. Personnel probably identical to that shown in the other Bennie Moten photo. (Photo courtesy of Duncan Schiedt)

The now-legendary Joe "King" Oliver, best remembered today as the "discoverer" of Louis Armstrong, was once a fine New Orleans conetist who unfortunately was on a downhill slide toward poverty and oblivion when, in 1926, he led this 10-piece band, known as *KING OLIVER AND HIS DIXIE SYNCOPATORS*. In 1926 and '27, the group cut a few phonograph recordings for Vocalion and played some night clubs, primarily in Chicago. Soon afterward, in New York City, pianist Luis Russell assumed leadership of the group, leaving King Oliver to continue his lonely way until death overtook him, in Savannah, Georgia, in April, 1938. (Photo by courtesy of Bertrand Demeusy)

A nostalgic reminder of the men's sportswear (*and* the transportation!) of the mid - 1920s, graphically provided by this view of the *ELI RICE BAND,* out of Milwaukee. (Photo by courtesy of John Miner)

Here is a real MYSTERY — a photo of a band the name of which has been forgotten even by Gus McClung, one of the sidemen shown in this photo! Saxophonist Harold Blanchard says that while he was never a part of this group, he recalls seeing this band at Harlem's venerable Renaissance Ballroom, and that its leader (fifth from left, front row) played a musical saw. He adds that the orchestra had an excellent vibes man, who pre-dated Lionel Hampton in exploiting and popularizing that instrument in the field of jazz and dance music. The guitarist, incidentally, is Gene Fields. (PHOTO BY COURTESY OF GUS MC CLUNG)

An exceedingly rare photo of a little-known big band of the World War I era—*ALLIE ROSS' BAND,* in a photo taken some time between 1918 and 1920. Note the ornate stage, with hammered copper "foliage" set off by contrasting metallic draping behind the band. (photo by courtesy of Eubie Blake)

LUIS RUSSELL'S BAND grew out of the last big band which the legendary trumpeter Joe "King" Oliver had been leading, up until 1927. Russell had been the pianist with that band, which was known then as the Dixie Syncopators. But while Oliver, ailing badly and suffering from a severe mouth infection, was unable to hold the group together, Russell proved able to discipline the band into a free-swinging outfit which successfully combined New Orleans and swing styles. Most famous of the Luis Russell recordings is "Saratoga Shout," cut by them for OKeh records, January 24, 1930, with Red Allen as featured trumpeter. Russell, who was born August 5, 1907 at Careening Cay, an island off Panama, died recently, in New York. Personnel (Partial): Henry "Red" Allen, trumpet ; Greeley Walton , sax; Paul Barbarin, drums; Charlie Holmes, sax.

Alabama-born *Lucius "Lucky" Millinder*, while not a musician, began leading a big band in about 1930, toured Europe soon after that and, in 1934, took over leadership of the Mills Blue Rhythm Band. From then until the middle-1940s, he fronted big bands rather steadily, which groups came to include, at one time or another, such sidemen as Dizzy Gillespie, John Kirby, Charlie Shavers, and countless other well known musicians. (Photo by courtesy of RCA Victor)

The year is 1920, and the *GEORGE MORRISON ORCHESTRA* is at the Albany Hotel. (Photo courtesy of George Morrison) PERSONNEL: FRANK HANDY, TRUMPET; LEO DAVIS, SAXES AND TRUMPET; (STANDING) ANDY KIRK, BASS AND TENOR SAXES; GEORGE MORRISON (STANDING), LEADER/VIOLINIST; MARY COLSTON AND DESDEMONA DAVIS, PIANISTS; LEE MORRISON, BANJO; EUGENE MONTGOMERY, DRUMMER/VOCALIST; CUTHBERT BYRD, TENOR SAX; EDWARD CALDWELL, TROMBONE.

If the white bandleader Paul Whiteman had a counterpart in the Negro music world, it was *WILBUR SWEATMAN*, whose big, semi-symphonic dance band parallelled in style that of Whiteman. Born in Brunswick, Missouri, February 7, 1881, Sweatman learned piano from his sister. Largely self-taught on violin and clarinet, he worked in a youth band in Kansas City, a large circus band, a minstrel group and, still later, in vaudeville, doing an act in which he played three clarinets at once! Sweatman organized an all-Negro orchestra in 1902, and was musical director of Chicago's Grand and Monogram theatres, 1908-11. A member of ASCAP from 1917 (the song writers' licensing agency), Sweatman led a band which made hundreds of phonograph records, particularly in the mid-1920s. His band's output of dance music, which had some peripheral connections with jazz, was a staid, concert-type of popular music — forebear of the type which today is dispensed by Henry Mancini and others of that ilk. (Photo by courtesy of Eubie Blake)

Fronting on State Street in Chicago, almost midway between 31st and 32nd Streets, once stood the great Vendome Theatre—the 700-seat movie palace where, from 1918 to 1927, ERSKINE TATE AND HIS VENDOME SYNCOPATORS rocked their audiences with twice-nightly jazz concerts. These hour-long programs, wedged between feature films, usually opened with light classical overtures, followed quickly by mighty and driving jazz, poured enthusiastically forth by the talented Tate Orchestra.

By 1921, when this photo was taken, Erskine Tate's band comprised 12 pieces, by 1924, 15. At one time or another the orchestra included among its personnel, such men as Freddie Keppard, Louis Armstrong, Earl Hines, Fats Waller, Buster Bailey and Omer Simeon.

Tate moved his great orchestra to the Metropolitan Theatre, in 1926, where he remained until 1930, when the virtual collapse of the Negro theatre orchestras hit Chicago.

PERSONNEL: (L to R) Harry Johnson, Fayette Williams, Erskine Tate, James Tate, Jimmy Bertrand, Alvin Fernandez, Adrian Robinson, Norvel Morton, Joseph McCutcheon, John Hare, Walter Dyet, Raymond Whitsell.

Leaning proudly against the instrument truck for the *J. Frank Terry* band is trumpeter Francis Williams, who owned the truck, which he purchased *new* April 10, 1934. By October 12 of the same year, the odometer had rolled beyond the 50,000-mile mark, an indication of how much territory was covered by many big bands, just in order to keep working. *(Photo by courtesy of Francis Williams)*

The J. Frank Terry Chicago Nightingales, in Cincinnati, Ohio, 1934. *(Photo by courtesy of Francis Williams)* PERSONNEL: (SEATED AT TABLE, L TO R) JOHN "ROCKS" MC CONNELL, TROMBONE; ALFRED GIBSON, ALTO/TENOR/BARITONE/CLARINET; J. FRANK TERRY, LEADER — TROMBONE; DICK VANCE, TRUMPET. (STANDING) HOWARD "BUNNY" FIELDS, BASS; PHIL KEEBLE, DRUMS; JAMES "SCORCH 'EM" WILLIS; FRANCIS "FEW" WILLIAMS, TRUMPET; HOWARD WATSON, PIANO; BILL CRUMP, REEDS; WILLIE LEWIS, TRUMPET.

FESS WHATLEY'S SCHOOL BAND, some time in the early 1920s. Included here are Teddy Hill, Paul Bascomb and Shelton Hemphill. Fess Whatley stands in the second row, at far left, holding trumpet. (Photo by courtesy of Fess Whatley)

On stage at the Cotton Club, Cincinnati, summer of 1934. Personnel identical with the other photo, except for addition of Bill Simpson, who stands next to bassist Howard Fields. Trumpeter Francis Williams describes Simpson as ''. . . entertainer deluxe and, sometimes, front man for the band.'' *(Photo by courtesy of Francis Williams)*

FESS WHATLEY'S VIBRA CATHEDRAL BAND, Birmingham, late 1930s. A more or less standard instrumentation for the period, this band helped to develop some important talent for other, more famous bands than that led by the kindly, patient Fess Whatley, whose band didn't cut records, and stayed close to Birmingham for most of its work. (Photo by courtesy of Fess Whatley) PERSONNEL: PAUL COMAN, TROMBONE, ARTHUR MILLER, JOHNNY GRIMES, FESS WHATLEY, TRUMPETS; ALTON "SNOOKIE" DAVENPORT, DRUMS; JAMES D. SWYNE, BASS; ALBERT JONES, VIBES; JOHN REED, WILTON ROBERTSON, J. L. LOWE, AMOS GORDON, SAXES. THE PIANIST IS MARY ALICE CLARKE, WHO ALSO DOUBLED ON VIBES AND VOCALS.

The 1924 version of the *Sam Wooding Orchestra* which cut in Berlin, Germany in 1925, a series of records for Vocalion, among which were "By the Waters of Minnetonka" and "Alabamy Bound." (Photo courtesy of Sam Wooding) PERSONNEL: GARVIN BUSHELL, LEAD ALTO SAX; GENE SEDRIC, SECOND TENOR SAX; WILLIE LEWIS, THIRD ALTO; BOBBY MARTIN, LEAD TRUMPET; MACEO EDWARDS, SECOND TRUMPET; TOMMY LADNIER, THIRD TRUMPET; HERBERT FLEMINGS, TROMBONE; JOHN WARREN, BASS/TUBA; JOHNNY MITCHELL, TENOR/BANJO; GEORGE HOWE, DRUMS; SAM WOODING, PIANO/LEADER.

156

"Cootie" Williams (His first name actually is Charles), who was born in Mobile Alabama, made his first professional appearance in the "Eagle Eye" Shields band, in Florida, back in the mid-1920s, coming to New York in 1928 with the Alonzo Ross band. After working briefly with the orchestras of Chick Webb and Fletcher Henderson, he joined Duke Ellington, in 1929, and stayed until 1940. Following a short stay with Benny Goodman, Williams started his own big band in 1941 and continued leading it until the late 1940s. (Photo by courtesy of INTERNATIONAL MUSICIAN)

Clarinetist/alto saxophonist FESS WILLIAMS AND HIS ROYAL FLUSH ORCHESTRA, about mid-April, 1929. This band, popular at the Savoy Ballroom, recorded a great many sides for Victor, among them the 1929 discs of "Here 'tis," "A Few Riffs," and "Hot Town." (Photo by Courtesy of Duncan Schiedt) PERSONNEL: (USUAL ORDER) DAVID "JELLY" JAMES, TROMBONE; KEN ROANE AND GEORGE TEMPLE, TRUMPETS; OLIVER BLACKWELL, BANJO; EMMANUEL CASAMORE, TUBA; LOCKWOOD LEWIS, ALTO; RALPH BEDELL, DRUMS; ANDY PENDLETON, BANJO; FELIX GREGORY, CLARINET/TENOR; PERRY SMITH, CLARINET/TENOR; HANK DUNCAN, PIANO. SEATED IS LEADER FESS WILLIAMS.

From 1939 to '40, pianist *Teddy Wilson* tried his hand at leading a big band, for which he wrote many of the arrangements. Although his was an excellent orchestra, its life span was regrettably brief, leaving Wilson's fame to rest largely upon his work as a pianist with the white clarinetist Benny Goodman, 1935-9. Besides working concert dates with Goodman since then, he had earlier rolled up a wealth of experience, in the 1920s and '30s, with the bands of Erskine Tate, Willie Bryant, Louis Armstrong and others. (Photo by courtesy of INTERNATIONAL MUSICIAN)

An early ragtime pianist, *Luckeyth "Luckey" Roberts* was a favorite high society bandleader of the 1920s. Said to be an early influence on Duke Ellington, Luckey is best remembered today as the composer of "Moonlight Cocktail" and, later, "Massachusetts." (Photo courtesy of Duncan Schiedt)

This is the 1925 *Billy Butler Orchestra,* which the following year, became the Savoy Bearcats. Once this photo (which the years have not treated too kindly) included bass horn player "Chink" Johnson. The backdrop behind the band is the rear of the bandstand at Harlem's Nest Club. The loving cup in the foreground was won by the band in a contest against Fletcher Henderson! (Photo courtesy of Demas Dean) PERSONNEL: (SEATED, L TO R) RAMON HERNANDEZ, TENOR SAX; BILLY BUTLER, VIOLIN AND ALTO SAX; JAMES REVEY, TROMBONE; GILBERT PARIS, TRUMPET. (STANDING, SAME ORDER): LEROY TIBBS, PIANO; ENGLEMAR CRUMMEL, ALTO SAX; WILLIE LYNCH, DRUMS; DEMAS DEAN, TRUMPET; JIMMY GREEN, BANJO.

Bandleader *CHIC CARTER*, a portrait found among the personal effects of a deceased Michigan ballroom operator. Nearly destroyed by the heirs to the estate were this and many other photos of bands and bandleaders which had been accumulated by the ballroom during its many years of operation.

An immensely popular trumpeter (and, to a lesser degree, singer/drummer/fluegelhornist) *ROY ELDRIDGE*, whose trumpet was an important voice in the bands of Horace Henderson, Zack Whyte, Speed Webb, Cecil Scott, McKinney's Cotton Pickers, Teddy Hill, Fletcher Henderson and others. He also has fronted some big bands of his own, in addition to which he has played in the otherwise white bands of Artie Shaw and Gene Krupa. (Photo courtesy Duncan Schiedt)

Composer/saxophonist *Joe Garland*, after a long period of work as a sideman with Elmer Snowden, Leon Abbey, Lucky Millinder, Don Redman and Louis Armstrong, took over the Luis Russell Orchestra at about the time when the U.S. entered World War II, and continued to work as a bandleader into the 1950s. Better remembered as a composer than a bandsman, Garland composed "Leap Frog" and "In the Mood," the latter a tune based upon a "riff" which had been earlier recorded as "Hot and Anxious" by Fletcher Henderson's Orchestra. Garland now lives in Teaneck, New Jersey. (Photo by courtesy of INTERNATIONAL MUSICIAN)

LOUIE!!!

THE GEORGE MORRISON ORCHESTRA, Phoenix, Arizona, 1919, its personnel including a couple of young people who later achieved both fame and fortune! (Photo by courtesy of George Morrison) PERSONNEL: CUTHBERT BYRD AND LEO DAVIS, SAXES; LEE MORRISON (LATE BROTHER OF THE BANDLEADER), BANJO; THEODORE MORRIS, TROMBONE; DESDEMONA DAVIS, PIANO; VIOLINIST/LEADER, GEORGE MORRISON. THE VOCALIST, (IN CASE YOU HAVEN'T GUESSED!) IS HATTIE MC DANIEL. SEATED AT RIGHT, WITH BASS SAX, IS FLEDGLING BANDLEADER ANDY KIRK, THE DRUMMER/VOCALIST IS EUGENE MONTGOMERY.

The Sweethearts of Rhythm, made up largely of Negro artists, and led by Anna Mae Winburn, produced some remarkably fine dance music, and developed a large following of fans, particularly among Harlem audiences. In the nine years that it existed following its establishment in Piney Wood, Mississippi, some time in 1940, this orchestra played in such top-flight New York spots as the Savoy Ballroom and the Apollo Theatre. Using arrangements chiefly from the pen of Maurice King, the band featured excellent charts of BODY AND SOUL, MAN WITH THE HORN, THREE 'BONES, and others. From 1949 to 1955 — after the demise of the Sweethearts of Rhythm as a big band — its leader continued to front small combos in supper clubs, recording several sides for Guild Records in 1954. (PHOTO COURTESY OF ANDY KIRK) PERSONNEL: (BOTTOM ROW, L TO R) JOHNNIE MAE RICE, PIANO; ANNA MAE WINBORN, LEADER; CARLENE MURRAY, FRANCES GADERSON, ELOISE ___, VIOLA BURNSIDE, WILLA MAE WONG, SAXES; JEAN TRAVIS, INA BYRD AND HELEN JONES, TROMBONES. (TOP ROW, L TO R) TRUMP MARGO, BASS; UNIDENTIFIED GUITARIST; PAULINE WILLIAMS, DRUMS; JEAN STARR, RAY CARTER, JOHNNIE MAE STANSBURY, TOBY BUTLER, TRUMPETS.

CHARLIE ELGAR'S CREOLE BAND was not only a leading Chicago band of the post-World War I era, but was an "incubator" for talent from which many another orchestra drew sidemen. Elgar, whose band was a favorite at Chicago's old Savoy Ballroom, later moved to the Dreamland Ballroom, in the same city, where he expanded the orchestra to 15 pieces and remained for some six years afterward. (PHOTO COURTESY OF BERTRAND DEMEUSY) PERSONNEL: LEFT TO RIGHT: ELGAR (STANDING, AT PHONOGRAPH); LEROY BRADSHAW, DRUMS/XYLOPHONE/MARIMBA; WM. SHELBY, BANJO/GUITAR; WALTER WRIGHT, BASS; WALTER GOSSETTE, PIANO/ORGAN; WM. NEELEY, TENOR/FLUTE; WM. RANDALL, TRUMPET; BERT HALL, TENOR/EUPHONIUM; HARRY SWIFT, TROMBONE; RICHARD CURRY, DRUMS; JOE SUDLER, TRUMPET; CLIFFORD KING, CLARINET/ALTO; DARNELL HOWARD, ALTO/SOPRANO/CLARINET.

167

Another of the many important "runners up" for fame and fortune in the big band world: *ZACK WHYTE AND HIS CHOCOLATE BEAU BRUMMELS,* a Midwestern band which alternated largely between New York and Chicago. Sy Oliver, later to reach fame as one of the chief arrangers for Jimmie Lunceford, was a trumpeter in Whyte's band of the late 1920s and very early 30s. (Photo courtesy of Duncan Schiedt)

ZACK WHYTE & HIS CHOCOLATE BEAU BRUMMELS
Jan. 22, 24 & 27, Tue., Thur., Sun. Mat.
CRYSTAL DANSANT

CHAPTER XXVIII

Can The Big Bands Return?

A question commonly asked by those who loved the sounds of the big dance bands is "Will the big bands return?" Behind this question, however, is the more basic query, "Is it POSSIBLE for the big bands to return?"

If this seems vague, consider this example: We might cry out all that we wished—even great numbers of us—for a healthy return to the days when America was covered with great tracts of virgin forestlands, when there were miles of unsullied wilderness. But the truth is that we just can't do so. That is an era gone forever.

If this analogy seems remote from the question, "Will the big bands return?", consider this fact:

Most of the so-called experts who say flatly that we cannot have a revival of such orchestras usually present their major argument somewhat as follows: The big bands can't come back, no matter how much the public clamors for them, because there are no more huge ballrooms where such bands could play.

Such a statement seems true enough, if one examines it superficially. It's true that Frank Daley's Meadowbrook is gone. So is the Glen Island Casino. The Savoy Ballroom, which held out bravely until the late 1950s, is no more. Two major ballrooms in Michigan, one at Fruitport, the other at Walled Lake, burned to the ground some time ago.

Inside the present-day Statler-Hilton Hotel (once the Hotel Pennsylvania) the room that was the big happy Cafe Rouge has long since been sliced through with partitions which so reduced its size that a quartet would seem large.

Most of the nation's amusement parks—almost all of which featured a hulking wooden ballroom—are gone forever.

Only a handful of ballrooms still operate: The Steel Pier at Atlantic City, Hershey Park, Elitch's Garden in Denver. But not many more.

Whether the band is Negro or white doesn't matter now. Opportunities for the big dance bands have been sharply curtailed—by a paucity of ballrooms, by high labor costs, by tremendous travel expenses, by the collective refusal of many American musicians to travel interminably and to live out of suitcases as once they did.

But does this really prove that the big bands cannot come back into vogue—if the public wants them?

To answer this, let's consider what became of many ballrooms. They were often turned into warehouses, supermarkets, roller rinks, or bowling alleys.

If a dancing public were to encourage big bands to reappear on the scene—by purchasing recordings by such aggregations, requesting big band selections of their radio stations and most importantly, *buying tickets* to concerts and dances featuring such groups, those same warehouses, supermarkets, roller rinks and bowling alleys could quickly metamorphose into ballrooms again.

After all, our overabundance of supermarkets is all too apparent from the very competition which forces them to operate in many cases on a mere 1% profit.

Bowling alleys were among the highest business fatalities of recent years. Owners of a good many ten pin parlors would likely welcome a chance to substitute a polished dance floor for a battery of guttered Brunswick alleys.

As for roller rinks, they lend themselves handsomely to nearly instant changeover to ballroom status, with a minimal investment.

And even in this age of high construction costs, a fairly adequate 50 ft. x 150 ft. ballroom can *still* be erected for less than $100,000*—a ballroom

*A minimal figure quoted June, 1966, by a large southern architectural firm.

which unlike those of yesteryear would be comfortably air conditioned, and need not rely upon the fickle breezes from some nearby lake for a welcome relief from the heat which is so inevitable in crowded dance halls.

It would appear, then, that big bands could come back, if only the public were to demand them. And surely good public acceptance would provide the funds necessary to make such bands profitable. (A 15-piece band can even now operate profitably on a minimum gross take of around $6,500 weekly).

If we want big bands, the Negro bands would surely be in greater evidence, would come to much greater fame than they did during the time of Chick Webb, McKinney's Cotton Pickers, and all the other fine aggregations of days long gone.

This presumption derives in part from the Civil Rights movement of recent years, and in part from a natural, if slow, process of integration and racial acceptance which long has been operating to the favor of Negroes in general, and Negro musicians in particular.

Today the American dance scene is open to the Negro as never before. The bandstands are open to the colored man with musical ability, and the dance floors are open to those of his race who would dance.

If the era of the great Negro band should return, more doors than ever would open wide—providing that there is an eager, dancing public waiting just beyond those doors!

In spite of rising construction costs, a *BALLROOM* similar to this large skating rink can still be erected at a reasonable cost, utilizing a pre-constructed steel building to which a decorative facade is added. (Photo Courtesy of BUTLER MANUFACTURING COMPANY)

Dates and Places of Births

ARMSTRONG, LOUIS—7/4/00, New Orleans, La.

BASIE, WILLIAM "COUNT"—8/21/04, Red Bank, New Jersey

BLAKE, EUBIE—2/7/83, Baltimore, Maryland

BRYANT, WILLIE—8/30/08, New Orleans, La.

CALLOWAY, CAB—12/24/07, Rochester, New York

CARTER, BENNY—8/8/07, New York City, N.Y.

COLUMBUS, CHRIS—6/17/03, Atlantic City, N.J.

COOK (E), DOC—9/3/91, Louisville, Kentucky

CREATH, CHARLIE—12/30/90, Ironton, Missouri

ECKSTINE, BILLY—7/8/14, Pittsburgh, Pa.

ELDRIDGE, ROY—1/30/11, Pittsburgh, Pa.

ELLINGTON, DUKE—4/29/99, Washington, D.C.

EUROPE, JAMES—2/22/81, Mobile, Alabama

FITZGERALD, ELLA—4/25/18, Newport News, Va.

GARLAND, JOE—8/15/07, Norfolk, Va.

GILLESPIE, DIZZY—10/21/17, Cheraw, South Carolina

HAMPTON, LIONEL—4/12/13, Louisville, Kentucky

HANDY, W. C.—11/16/73, Florence, Alabama

HAWKINS, COLEMAN—11/21/04, St. Joseph, Missouri

HAWKINS, ERSKINE—7/26/14, Birmingham, Alabama

HENDERSON, FLETCHER—12/18/98, Cuthbert, Georgia

HENDERSON, HORACE—1904, Cuthbert, Georgia

HILL, TEDDY—12/7/09, Birmingham, Alabama

HINES, EARL—12/28/05, Duquesne, Pa.

HITE, LES—1/13/03, DuQuoin, Ill.

HOPKINS, CLAUDE—8/24/06, Washington, D.C.

JACKSON, DEWEY—6/21/00, St. Louis, Mo.

JETER, JAMES—8/10/03, Little Rock, Arkansas

JOHNSON, BUDDY—1/10/15, Darlington, S. C.

JOHNSON, CHARLIE—11/21/91, Philadelphia, Pa.

JORDAN, LOUIS—7/8/08, Brinkley, Arkansas

KIRK, ANDY—5/28/98, Cincinnati, Ohio (or possibly Newport, Ky.)

LEONARD, HARLAN—1904, Kansas City, Mo.

LUNCEFORD, JIMMIE—6/6/02, Fulton, Missouri

MARABLE, FATE—12/2/90, Paducah, Kentucky

McKINNEY, WM.—1894, Paducah, Kentucky

McSHANN, JAY—1/12/09, Muskogee, Oklahoma

MILLINDER, LUCKY—8/8/00, Anniston, Alabama

MORRISON, GEORGE—9/9/91, Fayette, Mo.

MOTEN, BENNIE—11/13/94, Kansas City, Mo.

OLIVER, KING—5/11/85, Abend, Louisiana

REDMAN, DON—7/29/00, Piedmont, West Virginia

ROBERTS, LUCKEY—8/7/95, Philadelphia, Pa.

RUSSELL, LUIS—8/5/02 (b. at Careening, Cay, an island near Panama)

SISSLE, NOBLE—8/10/89, Indianapolis, Indiana

SWEATMAN, WILBUR—2/7/82, Brunswick, Missouri

TATE, ERSKINE—12/19/95, Memphis, Tennessee

TRENT, ALPHONSO—8/24/05, Ft. Smith, Arkansas

WALLER, FATS—5/21/04, New York City, N.Y.

WEBB, CHICK—2/10/02, Baltimore, Maryland

WEBB, SPEED—7/18/11, Peru, Indiana

WILLIAMS, COOTIE—7/24/08, Mobile, Alabama

WILLIAMS, FESS—4/10/94, Danville, Kentucky

WILSON, TEDDY—11/24/12, Austin, Texas

Theme Songs

Fletcher Henderson	CHRISTOPHER COLUMBUS
Duke Ellington	TAKE THE "A" TRAIN (N.B., earlier, the band used as a theme EAST ST. LOUIS TOODLE OO)
Count Basie	ONE O' CLOCK JUMP
Chick Webb	LET'S GET TOGETHER
Ella Fitzgerald	A TISKET, A TASKET
Andy Kirk & His Clouds of Joy	UNTIL THE REAL THING COMES ALONG (Closing theme: CLOUDS)
Erskine Hawkins	TUXEDO JUNCTION
Don Redman	CHANT OF THE WEED
Jeter-Pillars	LAZY RHYTHM
Cab Calloway	MINNIE THE MOOCHER
Jimmie Lunceford	WHITE HEAT
Earl "Fatha" Hines	DEEP FOREST
McKinney's Cotton Pickers	CHERI (CHERRY)
Doc Cooke	BLAME IT ON THE BLUES
Elmer Calloway	SONG OF INDIA
Claude Hopkins	I WOULD DO ANYTHING FOR YOU
Blanche Calloway	GROWLIN' DAN
Willie Bryant	IT'S OVER BECAUSE WE'RE THROUGH
J. Frank Terry	IN THE GARDEN OF THE SUN
Fats Waller	AIN'T MISBEHAVIN'
Speed Webb	LOW SPEED (also known as SPIDER'S WEBB)
Fess Williams	MAKE ME KNOW IT!

Index of Pictures

Roseland Ballroom 10, 13, 16

The Band Bus 14

Jitterbugs of the 1940s 14, 15

New York City 16

Streckfus Liner J. S. 18

The Fate Marable Orchestra 18

James Reese Europe Orchestra 20

Fletcher Henderson Orchestra 22

Doc Cook and His Doctors
  of Syncopation 26

Charles L. Cook 27

Doc Cook's Dreamland Orchestra 27

Duke Ellington 28, 32, 33, 34, 35

The Ellingtonians 30

Duke Ellington and Band 30, 36

Johnny Hodges 32

Leon Abbey 34

McKinney's Cotton Pickers 38

Alphonso Trent 40

Alphonso Trent and Band 43, 46

Lena Horne 44, 104

Noble Sissle and his Orchestra 46

Jimmy Rushing 48

Billie Holiday 51

Count Basie and Orchestra 52, 55

Count Basie 53, 54

"Speed" Webb 56

Speed Webb's "Blue Devils" 59

Big Band advertising 60

"Pops" Armstrong 62

Louis Armstrong and Orchestra 63

Louis Armstrong 64, 102, 164

The Famous Ballroom, The Savoy 67

Chick Webb 67

Chick Webb and Orchestra 68

Ella Fitzgerald Orchestra 70, 72

Ella Fitzgerald 71, 102

Ella Fitzgerald and Illinois Jacquet 72

Fats Waller 74

Lena Horne and Fats Waller 75

Fats Waller's Big Band 76

Andy Kirk and his Clouds of Joy . . . 80, 91

Andy Kirk's Clouds of Joy 82

Andy Kirk 81

Erskine Hawkins and Orchestra 85

Bob Range, Erskine Hawkins'
  Trombonist 86

Erskine Hawkins 87, 90

Haywood Henry, associate of
  Erskine Hawkins 88

Jimmie Mitchell, Vocalist/Saxophonist
  for Erskine Hawkins 89

Don Redman 92, 95

Don Redman and Band 94, 96

James Jeter and Hayes Pillars:
  The Jeter-Pillars Band 99

Lionel Hampton 100, 102

Composer Otto Cesana conducting the
  Lionel Hampton Orchestra 102

Cab Calloway's Big Band with
  Lena Horne 104

Cab Calloway's Band 105, 107

Singer June Richmond 106

Claude Hopkins Orchestra 108, 110

The Jimmy Lunceford Orchestra   113, 114

Jimmy Lunceford 113

Sy Oliver 114

Harlan Leonard 117

Harlan Leonard Orchestra 117

Earl Hines 118, 121

Earl Hines Band 121

Dizzy Gillespie 122

Leon Abbey's Band 130, 131

Jap Allen & his group 131

Walter Barnes & his Royal Creolians   132

Eubie Blake 132

Tiny Bradshaw & his Orchestra 133

Eubie Blake's Shuffle Along Band 133

Willie Bryant's Orchestra 134

W. C. Handy 134

Benny Carter 135

"The Mad Men", a part of the Chris
  Columbus Big Band 136

Chic Carter Orchestra 136

Billy Eckstine 137

Marion Hardy & his Alabamians 138

Duke Ellington's son Mercer, trumpeter,
  composer, arranger & bandleader . . . 139

Coleman Hawkins 140

Les Hite 141

The Teddy Hill Band 141

Doc Hyder Orchestra 142

The Alex Jackson Orchestra 142

Dewey Jackson Peacock Orchestra 143

Buddy Johnson 143

Louis Jordan 144

Milton Larkins and his Orchestra 144

The George E. Lee Novelty Singing
  Orchestra 145

(Irving) Mills Blue Rhythm Band 145

Charlie Creath's Band 146

Bennie Moten Orchestra 147, 148

King Oliver and his Dixie Syncopators   148

Eli Rice Band 149

Gus McClung with a band 149

Allie Ross' Band 150

Luis Russell's Band 150

Lucius "Lucky" Millinder 151

George Morrison Orchestra 151, 165

Wilbur Sweatman 152

174

Erskine Tate and his Vendome
    Syncopators 153

Francis Williams of the
    J. Frank Terry Band 154

The J. Frank Terry Chicago
    Nightingales. 154

Fess Whatley's School Band 155

Fess Whatley's Vibra Cathedral Band   156

Sam Wooding Orchestra 156

Charles "Cootie" Williams 157

Fess Williams and his Royal
    Flush Orchestra 158

Teddy Wilson, pianist 159

Luckeyth "Luckey" Roberts 160

Billy Butler Orchestra 160

Chic Carter 161

Roy Eldridge. 162

Joe Garland. 163

The Sweethearts of Rhythm 166

Charlie Elgar's Creole Band 167

Zack Whyte and Band 168